the total temple makeover

about the author

Gregory L. Jantz, PhD, is a popular speaker and award-winning author. He is a certified chemical-dependency professional, a licensed mental-health counselor, and a nationally certified eating-disorder specialist. Dr. Jantz is the founder and executive director of the Center for Counseling and Health Resources, a leading mental-health and chemical-dependency treatment facility, with four clinics in the Seattle area.

The Center is a full-service counseling organization, which also acts as a referral and information source for those seeking help for a variety of mental-health issues. The Center specializes in whole-person care, with individuals from across the United States and internationally coming to participate in the hope-filled work of recovery. Dr. Jantz's whole-person approach addresses the emotional, relational, intellectual, physical, and spiritual dimensions of each person, with a uniquely tailored treatment plan. Over the course of the past twenty years, Dr. Jantz and the Center have treated nearly seven thousand people with all types of disorders, using the successful whole-person approach.

His compassionate, solution-oriented viewpoints on timely topics, plus a natural gift for storytelling, make him a sought-after guest on local and national radio and television. He speaks nationally at conferences, seminars, and retreats on a wide variety of topics, utilizing his extensive expertise and experience. Dr. Jantz has also hosted several popular live call-in radio shows, participating in well over a thousand individual interviews since 1995.

Dr. Jantz hosts a monthly audiotape club, the Hope and Help series, on the topic of healing and recovery. This resource is sent monthly to subscribers from across the United States and provides cutting-edge nutritional information, new advances in the treatment of eating disorders and addictions, inspiration to aid healing, and practical suggestions for ongoing recovery.

Dr. Jantz and his wife, LaFon, have been married for twenty years and are blessed with two children, Gregg and Benjamin.

For further information on the Center for Counseling and Health Resources, go to: www.aplaceofhope.com

or

The Center, Inc.
PO Box 700
547 Dayton Street
Edmonds, WA 98020
Nationwide toll free 888-771-5166
Fax 425-670-2807

the total temple makeover

how to turn YOUR BODY

into a TEMPLE

you can REJOICE in

dr. gregory jantz

with ann mcmurray

HOWARD
PUBLISHING CO.

Our purpose at Howard Publishing is to:
- Increase *faith* in the hearts of growing Christians
- Inspire *holiness* in the lives of believers
- Instill *hope* in the hearts of struggling people everywhere
  Because He's coming again!

the total temple makeover © 2005 by Dr. Gregory Jantz
All rights reserved. Printed in the United States of America
Published by Howard Publishing Co., Inc.
3117 North 7th Street, West Monroe, Louisiana 71291-2227
www.howardpublishing.com

05 06 07 08 09 10 11 12 13 14   10 9 8 7 6 5 4 3 2 1

Edited by Ramona Cramer Tucker and Susan Duncan Wilson
Cover design by Terry Dugan Design
Interior design by Gabe Cardinale
Author photo by Randy DeMoss, DeMoss Photography

Library of Congress Cataloging-in-Publication Data

Jantz, Gregory L.
    The total temple makeover : how to turn your body into a temple you can rejoice in /
Gregory Jantz.
      p. cm.
    ISBN 1-58229-411-9
    1. Health—Religious aspects—Christianity. 2. Health behavior. I. Title.

RA776.J33 2005
613.2'5—dc22
                                              2004060698

DEDICATION

TO LARRY ACORD—
A man of God and a gentle soul in a giant's body. Health problems and obesity took him at the age of forty-nine. It was his wish that no one ever have to endure what he endured. It is my hope that the words in these pages can help fulfill his wish.

AND

TO TERRY ACORD, LARRY'S BROTHER—
Who, after watching his brother suffer, poured his heart into the realization of this project of hope. His deepest desire was to honor his brother's wishes.

This is how we know that we love the children of God: by loving God and carrying out his commands.
—1 John 5:2

CONTENTS

Table of Recipes

INTRODUCTION

KALE'S STORY—and Yours

KALE'S STORY

Sundays were always my favorite day of the week. We would go to church and sit together as a family—four generations of us. We had been one of the founding families of that church. Dad and Grandpa had helped to lay the stones, build the walls, and even shingle the roof. It was a place where God's family met together— a place where we all felt we belonged.

After church we would gather at my grandparents' farmhouse for dinner. The smells that came from that kitchen! Thick, juicy ham, mashed potatoes covered with gravy, delicious homemade rolls and hand-churned butter, fresh vegetables from the garden—it all seemed to flow from that kitchen like a bounty from heaven itself. We would eat until we were stuffed, with more than one man in the family having to loosen his belt in recognition of the wonderful meal.

Afterward we would gather in the living room. Most of the men would nap; the women would meet at the piano to sing favorite hymns. It was the one day we all seemed like family.

No one yelled. No one was angry.

And no one called me fat.

Since you are reading this book, it's a fair assumption that you have three things in common with Kale and most other readers:

- ◆ You strive to follow a Christian life.
- ◆ You struggle with a weight issue.
- ◆ You feel guilty.

After all, why should you as a Christian struggle with weight issues? Does your struggle mean you're not "spiritual" enough? Shouldn't the self-discipline that comes with following and obeying God equip you to say no to a hot-fudge sundae? If you're such a great Christian, why aren't you a thin Christian?

Part of the answer, of course, is that as hard as we try, none of us are "great" Christians. We are striving, falling, groping, stumbling-in-the-dark Christians who need God's assistance on a day-to-day—even a moment-by-moment—level. We have our periods of successes . . . and our times of failure. Our very human nature, thanks to Adam and Eve way back in the Garden, ensures that we're imperfect. And that lack of perfection manifests itself in a variety of ways—including our body weight.

Another part of the answer is that we tend to associate God only with the intangible things, the spiritual aspect of our lives. We think, whether on a conscious or subconscious level: "God is somebody we talk to on Sunday; He isn't around when I'm standing in the mall choosing between a fat-free pretzel and a Double Doozie chocolate chip cookie. He is worried about my soul, not my cholesterol count. Right?"

Wrong. God, who created us, cares about all aspects of our lives—spiritual, mental, and physical. Yet we do not seem to seek His guidance as we make choices about how we treat our bodies. We treat our physical health as less important than our mental and spiritual health.

But God Himself calls our bodies His temple and makes it clear that He wants us to take care of them: "Do you not know that your body is a temple of the Holy Spirit, who is in you, whom you have received from God? You are not your own; you were bought at a price. Therefore honor God with your body" (1 Corinthians 6:19–20).

Your body is the only "house" you have all the years you are on this earth. It isn't until we are taken to heaven and transformed that we receive a different sort of house. So why not make the body you have right now the absolute healthiest body possible?

Almost all of us would like to have a healthier body.

The trouble comes when we try to do something about it. We get frustrated and think, "I've tried everything, and nothing works. If God wants me to be healthy, then why doesn't He help? Why isn't losing weight, balancing my food intake, and exercising easier?"

The Total Temple Makeover is designed to make it easier. It's a twelve-week program for real people who are struggling with weight issues. In three months not only can you transform your body into a healthier temple, you can change your lifestyle and thinking—the only way to insure that your weight loss is permanent.

Over the last twenty years, after helping thousands at the Center for Counseling and Health Resources in Seattle, I've found that quick fixes always lead to disappointment and pain. I'm more convinced than ever that treating the whole person is the only approach that gives whole health. No matter how many times you've tried (and I've worked with people who've been overweight most of their lives), I want you to know that there is hope. Really.

But it isn't enough to be at a healthy weight; you have to learn to live at a healthy weight.

Is this doable? Yes! Many have undertaken this program and succeeded. Each of them stepped out in faith, hoping for success, yet fearful of another failure.

Take Karen, for example. Her entire being seemed to revolve around her three children's needs. She desperately wanted to be thinner, but the pounds continued to creep onto her five-foot-four-inch frame. Always considered chunky as a child, Karen was, as an adult, fast approaching obese. After a particularly difficult shopping trip, where she couldn't find any clothes to fit her, Karen realized she just had to lose weight. She wanted a fast-track diet. Instead, the Center helped her focus on health, rather than weight; on long-term, rather than short-term; on nutrition, rather than calories. Today Karen has returned to a healthy weight. She no longer is obsessed with being thin, but has learned to appreciate her body—not as a physical representation of who she is, but as the temple given to her by God to serve Him and her family. She's healthy, she's happy, and she's free from bondage to her flesh.

When Mike started on the program, his concern wasn't his weight. It was his health. The report from his annual physical was sobering. "If you don't do something different, you're headed for serious health problems," this forty-three-year-old was told. It came as a bit of a shock to Mike that something he thought was OK needed "fixing." It didn't help that he really didn't want to do anything different; Mike was content with his life and his habits. So he fought the doctor's advice. One day, however, he realized that his struggle with weight was simply a mirror of an ongoing spiritual struggle. When Mike was able to frame his weight problem as a spiritual battle, he was able to surrender his weight to God's sovereignty. Now, day by day, Mike is winning by giving the battle over to the Lord.

Like Karen and Mike, you have to come to a personal decision to allow God to take over your battle with weight and make the temple He has blessed you with the healthiest one possible. This requires a change in focus, awareness, priorities, and trust. Can you give yourself three months? Can you dedicate yourself to health for the next twelve weeks?

This book is divided into twelve chapters, to fit the twelve weeks of this program. Each chapter has seven sections:

1. Inspiration
2. Devotional
3. Thoughts for Food
4. What You Eat
5. The Journey Journal

6. Make It Real
7. A Voice along the Path

You can choose to read the chapter in one sitting once a week, or you can read one section each day of the week, depending on your schedule, temperament, and preference. Either way is fine. Along the way you'll find practical advice, encouragement, specific tips to help you understand what you're eating (and why), and exercises (don't groan yet—they're not as bad as you think!). You'll also get a sneak peek at the thoughts of Kale, a person who is also walking through the program.

Are you ready for a healthier body? The time to start is now.

Let's do it—together!

If anyone is in Christ, he is a new creation; the old has gone, the new has come!

—2 Corinthians 5:17

TRANSFORMATION
week 1
d a y 1

INSPIRATION: The Journey Begins

Imagine this scene: Someone hands you a magic pill that has the power to instantly drop you to your desired weight. The catch is, you can take only one during your lifetime.

Would you take it now?

If so, how long do you think the weight loss would last?

Study after study has proven that quick-fix diets don't work. Even if you are able to achieve the desired weight loss, it isn't permanent. Why is that?

If you understand that we are all made up of three "selves"—the physical self, the mental self, and the spiritual self—the answer becomes obvious. The problem with treatments like liposuction, protein diets, etc., is that they treat only the physical self.

Medical science can remove five liters of fat from the body, but it can't cosmetically reshape the spirit and self-image. Protein diets can starve the body's weight down, but they can't reshape the heart and mind.

A healthy life means changing not only the way we feed ourselves but also the way we think and feel about ourselves.

For the Christian this is particularly difficult. After all, you are the child of God—the God who created the universe and loved you enough to send His Son to die for you. So why can't He instantly peel off a few lousy pounds for you?

Yes, God *could* do that, but He doesn't.

Why? Because He loves you.

Just like quick-fix diets, surgery, etc., don't provide lasting results for most, neither would miraculous weight loss. God's answer leads to a permanent fix—a transformation—one that includes mind, body, and spirit to bring you closer to becoming the person God knows you can be.

Will it be simple? Of course not.

Will there be obstacles? Certainly.

Will you fall backward at times along the path? Most assuredly.

But keep in mind, this is a journey, not a race. The *destination* is the important thing here, not the speed. I want to measure progress, not performance.

Getting Started

As you go through the exercises on the following pages, you'll begin to set goals for yourself. Afterward you may look at those goals and say, "Impossible! I'll never lose that much."

At this stage, doubt is understandable. Remember, though, that being a child of God enables you to take that first step of faith, even if you don't know where it will lead. Like a child learning to walk, those first baby steps might be hard, but have faith! The destination is worth it. And your body deserves it!

As we take these first critical steps together, I'm going to make you a promise: I don't know how many years you've lived with the pain of weight and body-image issues, but I do know that your remaining years can be healthier and happier ones.

All I ask is that you give the next twelve weeks the best of your time and energy.

- I ask you to try to follow the advice in these pages.
- I ask you to learn and apply what you've learned.
- And I ask you to believe.

If you can do that for the next three months, I *guarantee* God will bring about some amazing changes in your life!

week 1

d a y 2

DEVOTIONAL: One Step at a Time

WHAT'S ON YOUR FRIDGE?

Write the verse below on a piece of paper and post it on your refrigerator door. Do the same each week, adding a new scripture to the old ones already posted. Read them every time you are tempted to open the door of the fridge and reach for that unhealthy food you're craving.

> I can do everything through him who gives me strength. (Philippians 4:13)

Determining to undo the consequences of overeating can be overwhelming, but remember: you don't have to lose twenty pounds, forty pounds, or even a hundred pounds today to be successful.

Today you simply have to eat well.

Today you need to pull away from the table with something left on your plate.

Today you need to engage in a physical activity you enjoy.

Today you need to set your sights on losing that first pound.

Simply take care of today, and take this journey one forward step at a time. And as you take that first baby step, know that you are not alone. Others have walked this path before and emerged with a healthier body and lifestyle. And all of you reading this book are right now walking the same path. You have lots of company on your journey!

Most of all, a Father who loves you just as you are today will be right beside you on the road.

Throughout the week, use this prayer as your strength. You may even want to mark this page so you can return to it easily.

Heavenly Father,

There are so many places, so many ways in which my life is not as it should be. You see and know all. You know how I fall short at times, how weak I can be. In particular, You know my struggles with my body and weight. This day I lay the burden of being overweight at Your feet, Lord. I acknowledge that I cannot overcome it alone— I need one greater than myself to help me over this mountain.

Lord, You are greatest of all. Nothing is beyond Your power and will. Give me the strength to change who and what I am. I ask that You help me grow in mind, spirit, and body to achieve more than I ever thought I could.

Help me to walk this path with patience, with endurance, and with my eyes on You. Amen.

week 1
d a y 3

THOUGHTS FOR FOOD: *Diet* Redefined

One of the first things you need to do is throw away the typical definition of *diet*. Most people use the word to refer to a period of forced hunger to reduce what they weigh. But in this book, I'll only use the word *diet* in its original sense—the lifestyle you choose in terms of the types of foods you eat, how you prepare them, when you eat them, and how you combine them. In other words, I'll talk about your diet, not a diet.

EATING LIKE A BIRD WON'T HELP YOU GROW WINGS

You've seen the magazine headlines:

- ◆ "The Diets of the Stars!"
- ◆ "Eat like a Supermodel"
- ◆ "10 Easy Steps to That Drop-Dead Figure—Guaranteed"

Look, even if I could sit beside supermodel Tyra Banks for the rest of my life, eat the same foods, take a bite only when she does, and do the same workouts, I won't look anything like Tyra Banks! There's also a little thing called *genetics* that comes into play.

Part of the journey to a healthier body and life means that you learn to accept the way God made you *without* accepting the idea that you have to be overweight. Yes, maybe God gave you one blue eye and one brown or a nose that you think is too big. However, God didn't force that Little Debbie cake on your plate, and He didn't create the resulting extra padding around your thighs. That came from the choice you made.

And that's why, as we talk about choices, I'll ask you to make one change in your eating habits each week. Here is the first one.

Ready?

CHANGE YOUR HABITS!

New Habit #1: Think water—the most important "food" for your body.

Technically, water is not a food since it has no nutritional value. However, it is a known fact that you die much more quickly of thirst than of starvation. Making sure your body is properly hydrated is the cornerstone of healthy eating.

How much water do you need? Most overweight people do not drink enough water—they substitute high-sugar drinks, coffee, and alcoholic beverages. Make the commitment now to drink two to three quarts of water a day while you are going through this program. If you buy the one liter water bottles (16.9 oz.), that means drinking four to six water bottles per day. Plan to have one upon rising in the morning, one about twenty to thirty minutes before each meal, one during the three meals, and one bottle at a time of your choice. Avoid drinking a lot of water near bedtime, especially if you visit the bathroom several times at night. Becoming sleep deprived won't help you accomplish your goal and brings other problems of its own.

The benefits of proper hydration are too numerous to mention. Your skin, hair, organs, digestion—practically every body part and function—benefit from the proper amount of water. Drink natural spring water, when available, and consume it at a cool—not ice-cold—temperature.

To remind myself why I should drink water, I created my very own water bottle that lists the benefits of water right on it:

◆ Aids in fat metabolism
◆ Helps concentration
◆ Gives proper muscle tone

- ◆ Improves mood
- ◆ Regulates blood pressure
- ◆ Decreases water retention

With so many wonderful benefits, how could I not drink my water during the day? (If such a tool would be helpful to you, go to www.aplaceofhope.com or write to the address on page 236 for ordering information.)

So be encouraged! You can build healthier eating habits, one at a time. And I'll help. Soon you'll be able to apply the simple principles in this book without even thinking about them. They'll just be part of your lifelong "diet."

week 1
d a y 4

WHAT YOU EAT: Food Groups

Like many of you, I grew up with an understanding of "healthy eating" that was summarized in the four food groups.

THE FOUR FOOD GROUPS

The four food groups were developed in 1956 by the United States Department of Agriculture (USDA) as a way to promote balanced nutrition (see figure 1).

The Four Food Groups

Figure 1.

Their diagram basically recommended eating a mixture of four broad food groups. They were:

1. Meats, poultry, fish, dry beans and peas, eggs, and nuts
2. Dairy products; such as milk, cheese, and yogurt
3. Grains
4. Fruits and vegetables

The four food groups remained the foundation of what was considered nutritious eating until 1992. Then the Food and Drug Administration (FDA) introduced the now common Food Guide Pyramid (see figure 2). [1]

The Food Guide Pyramid

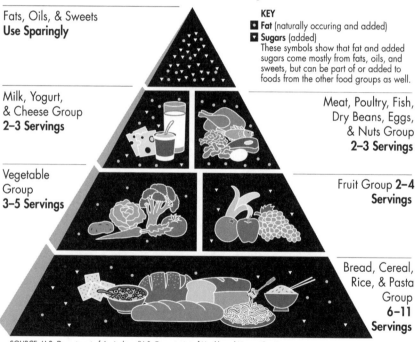

Fats, Oils, & Sweets
Use Sparingly

KEY
◼ **Fat** (naturally occuring and added)
▼ **Sugars** (added)
These symbols show that fat and added sugars come mostly from fats, oils, and sweets, but can be part of or added to foods from the other food groups as well.

Milk, Yogurt, & Cheese Group
2–3 Servings

Meat, Poultry, Fish, Dry Beans, Eggs, & Nuts Group
2–3 Servings

Vegetable Group
3–5 Servings

Fruit Group **2–4 Servings**

Bread, Cereal, Rice, & Pasta Group
6–11 Servings

SOURCE: U.S. Department of Agriculture/U.S. Department of Health and Human Services

Figure 2.

The food pyramid was supposed to address the biggest errors of the four food groups. Most specifically, it was intended to show how much of each type of food you should eat each day.

Immediately, however, the food pyramid came under attack. As our knowledge about nutrition evolves, there is a strong likelihood that the pyramid will be revised in the near future (we'll explore this in week 12), but it is a good basis for defining a balanced diet.

One of the greatest flaws of the food pyramid is that it places all the major food groups together. All grains are considered equal, as are all vegetables, fruits, fats, etc. We now know that this picture of the food groups is wrong, because in each category, there are "good" and "bad" types of foods. Although I'll explore each category in detail in later weeks, a brief discussion of the fat category will illustrate what I mean.

As you can see from the pyramid, fats are considered bad and should be used sparingly. But this view is simplistic, because different types of fats have very different effects on the body. Saturated fats—the primary fats that make up animal fat, dairy fat, and so on—are associated with increased heart risk. This is because they increase the levels of LDL cholesterol (the bad cholesterol you hear about in the news).

However, the fats found in unprocessed vegetable oils and, especially, olive oil have been found to reduce LDL levels. Yet they are treated the same in the pyramid as cow's butter.

THE AWE SYSTEM DEFINED

OK, you might be saying, I didn't pick up this book to become a nutritionist. I just want to eat healthier and lose weight.

And for that exact purpose I've created the AWE system.

What's the AWE system? The AWE system looks at each category of foods on the Food Guide Pyramid and breaks them down into three basic categories:

- ◆ Foods you should Avoid
- ◆ Foods you should Watch how much you consume
- ◆ Foods you are encouraged to Eat

Later on I'll direct you to sources for finding recipes and meal plans that follow the AWE system. No one intends to spend all their time counting calories or poring over food package information. But I want you to establish food purchasing and preparation habits, just as I want you to establish eating and exercise habits—habits that can become an automatic part of your life.

Keeping things simple is the most effective way to ensure lasting change.

week 1
d a y 5

THE JOURNEY JOURNAL: Your Starting Point

I know that many of us were taught not to write in books, but this book is made to write in. Most weeks I'll ask you to do some sort of writing on a worksheet that will help you in your journey toward a more healthy you.

In addition to what you write in this book, I want you to record your feelings, thoughts, and triumphs in a blank journal or a three-ring binder.

The appendices have several of the charts and graphs, which gives you the option of making copies of those pages to include in a three-ring binder, along with loose-leaf paper to record your extra writings. In the Journey Journal section, I'll give you suggestions each week for your journal writing.

Choose a time each day that works best for you to record events during your day and your thoughts about those events. Make sure to record episodes of impulsive/binge eating and the thoughts and feelings associated with those actions. This recorded account will allow you to look back at where you've been and how far you've come. You'll see the pitfalls, as well as wonderful victories.

Why is your journaling so important? So you can begin to identify patterns in your thoughts and actions. For example, do you tend to binge at certain times of the day? When interacting with certain people?

During certain activities, such as watching TV? It's important to begin gathering this data now so you can act on it in the weeks to come.

I can't stress enough how important this is. So don't just gloss over this section and keep reading. Make the commitment now to put together your journal. Take time to write. The information you will accumulate about yourself over the weeks will be invaluable in helping you reach your goal. It will be the foundation for changing your life.

If you'd like to share any stories or insights from your journal, I'd welcome them. Please send them to mystory@aplaceofhope.com. Your privacy will be maintained and respected. Just think—what you are learning may greatly help others as they travel toward a healthier life!

Whether you are following this program as a member of a group or on your own, you first need to define your starting point. After all, you can't start any journey without knowing where you currently are. So let's begin . . .

WORKSHEET: Where I Am Today

Today is _____

My weight is _____

My BMI is _____

(See appendix A, Body Mass Index, for how to calculate).

Fill in the blanks below with whatever enters your mind as you read the beginning words of the sentence. Don't stop to consider or worry about spelling, etc. Just write your honest responses.

I feel . . . _____

_____

_____

_____

_____

_____

_____

_____

I think . . . _____

_____

_____

_____

_____

_____

_____

_____

I hope . . . _____

_____

_____

_____

_____

_____

_____

Take some time to set up your journal or binder and begin your personal journaling there.

week 1
d a y   6

MAKE IT REAL: A Word about Weight

Although we want to track your weekly progress, it's important to keep in mind that what the scales say is only one gauge of measuring progress. In fact, it would be a good idea to put away your scales, except when you do your weekly weigh-in for your report. Constantly measuring the ups and downs of your body will only help feed the emotional roller coaster that helped you become overweight. So give your scales a "vacation" while you work on reshaping your life, and use them only to record your weekly progress.

WHEN TO WEIGH

When should you weigh yourself? It really doesn't matter, but you should strive to weigh yourself at the same day and time every week. This will help to keep the measurements consistent.

WHAT TO RECORD

More important than the raw numbers on the scale is recording how you feel physically and emotionally. In fact, if you would rather not measure weight and your Body Mass Index, or BMI (we'll talk soon about how to measure this), during the next ninety days, don't!

Trust what your body tells you—you will know if you feel better, are less bloated, and have more energy, etc. You don't need a scale to validate that you are getting healthier.

week 1
d a y 7

A VOICE ALONG THE PATH: Kale's Story

It's always easier to take a journey with someone else. Remember Kale, who loved Sundays as a child because it was the one day no one called him fat? Well, in this book you'll get to see his thoughts and impressions, struggles and joys. He'll be going through the same process along with you . . . and sharing candidly along the way.

Here is the beginning of Kale's story as he starts this twelve-week program.

Here we go again.

Another program, another disappointment. I've been asked to keep this journal as I start this program so that I can record my thoughts and feelings as I try to lose weight. So how am I feeling now? Frankly, I don't know why this program will be any different. I've lost track of the number of diet books and diet programs I've been on.

I don't even know why I keep trying. If L____ hadn't suggested I try it, I probably wouldn't bother, but I trust her opinion, and she was pretty insistent that it would help me. We'll see. But I don't have high hopes.

I guess the big reason I'm willing to try again is something that L____ said—how she felt that her weight problems were getting in the way of her progress as a Christian. I'd had an almost identical feeling lately that my weight problem was an ever-present, tangible measure of my inability to serve God as I should.

So here I am.

I'm not sure where I'm really going with this, where I should start, but I'm supposed to start tonight by simply praying for guidance and strength.

Lord, if I am truly to be Yours, then I can see that I need to be the master of my own body. Help me to find the strength, the power, to do what I know I should do. You know that I don't know what I'm supposed to do or how I'm supposed to do it.

I guess faith is like that—walking into the dark, trusting the One who walks beside you. The One who will be there with you at the end.

OK, Lord.

Here we go.

There *is* hope. Let's go together!

Ponder the path of thy feet, and let all thy ways be
established.

—Proverbs 4:26 KJV

CHARTING THE PATH

week 2

d a y 1

INSPIRATION: It's Your Choice

The verse from Proverbs that begins this chapter reminds us that no one should start a journey without knowing which road to take. No one starts building a house without a plan for how the finished product should look.

Yet when it comes to life, many of us treat the journey like a joyride. We simply travel down the highway—cursing the bumps and enjoying those straight stretches—until we run out of road.

Recall the story of the prodigal son and, in particular, this passage: "And not many days after the younger son gathered all together, and took his journey into a far country, and there wasted his substance with riotous living" (Luke 15:13 KJV).

We might not turn into complete hedonists like the prodigal son, but how many of us are squandering our gifts that God has given us? How many of us are wasting our "substance"?

Losing weight is like any other hard decision a Christian faces. We choose not to give in to peer pressure. We choose to accept the label of being different. We choose to know that when we stumble and fall, some will snicker behind our backs.

We choose this because we know that being a Christian isn't about perfection; it's about redemption.

Perhaps now is the time to reclaim a part of yourself you might have considered lost. Perhaps God will speak to your heart through this program, and in this small corner of your life, you will begin to choose a better path.

Place your faith in Him, but also realize that because you are His child, the power of His Spirit resides in you.

week 2

d a y 2

DEVOTIONAL: Trust in the Lord
WHAT'S ON YOUR FRIDGE?

> Trust in the LORD with all your heart and lean not on your own understanding; in all your ways acknowledge him, and he will make your paths straight. (Proverbs 3:5–6)

There is an old Hebrew prayer for travelers, called the *Tefillat haDerech*, that is fitting as you start down your own road this week. (Note: It is Hebrew tradition not to spell out the name of God, and we honor that tradition in the prayer below). Say it each night, and as you do, thank God for the good choices you have made that day. Then pray for strength and wisdom to make even more good choices the next day.

> *May it be Your will, Ad—, my God and God of my ancestors, to lead me, to direct my steps, and to support me in peace. Lead me in life, tranquil and serene, until I arrive at where I am going. Deliver me from every enemy, ambush, and hurt that I might encounter on the way and from all afflictions that visit and trouble the world. Bless the work of my hands. Let me*

receive divine grace and those loving acts of kindness and mercy in Your eyes and in the eyes of all those I encounter. Listen to the voice of my appeal, for You are a God who responds to prayerful supplication. Praised are You, Ad—, who responds to prayer.

week 2
d a y 3

THOUGHTS FOR FOOD: Realistic Expectations

What are the realistic expectations of changing your eating habits? Unfortunately, many of the promises made by advertisers are anything but realistic. Here are some of the headlines I found in a women's magazine:

- "Reach Your Dream Weight by Just Programming Your Brain for Weight Loss!"
- "The 7-Minute Secret That Melts Off 29 Pounds!"
- "Lose Weight on the 'Never Be Hungry' Diet"

(Ironically, right below the weight-loss title were these words: "Bake Up Some Happiness" with—you guessed it—chocolate cake, cookies, etc.)

What's wrong with us? Instead of the pounds melting off, somehow they are sneaking up behind us and latching on, because we keep gaining. Well, at least we know that we can "bake up some happiness," huh?

Sometimes, trying to set a realistic weight-loss goal seems almost impossible.

So what goals are realistic for you?

Well, you can expect to lose between one to two pounds a week by eating healthy.

You already know your current Body Mass Index from last week. Now look at appendix A on pages 213–14 again. To be at optimum health, you should be between 19 and 25 BMI. With one finger on your height, follow that line until you reach 19 BMI. Write down that weight. Then again follow the line until your finger reaches the cross point of 25 BMI. Write down that weight. This will give you your best weight range. Based on that range, calculate how much weight you have to lose (for encouragement's sake, you might want to try the 25 BMI number first). Divide that figure by one pound a week (for women) and two pounds a week (for men), and you will know approximately how many weeks you will need to reach your goal weight. Again, I want to stress that weight isn't gained overnight, nor is it lost overnight.

And now that I've told you all that, forget about it!

That's right—forget about it!

Am I crazy? Hardly. But I have a point to make. Just losing the weight doesn't change you into the healthy person you want to become. But changing the way you eat does.

Change Your Habits!

New Habit #2: Eat like the person you wish to become.

Make the commitment that today, right now, you are going to begin eating like the person you wish to become. For example, if you weigh 160 pounds and your goal is 125 pounds, then you need to start eating today as a healthy 125 pound person eats.

Here it comes, you're thinking. *This is where the pain starts.* Well, I have no doubt that reaching your weight goal will be trying for you. Let's face it, if it were easy, you wouldn't be reading this book. My focus, though, is not on how to make you suffer to achieve your goals. (Perhaps that's why so many weight-loss programs don't work. There's too much suffering involved!) However, I want to teach you how to make smart and creative decisions about substitutions, not sacrifices. The only sacrifice you need to consider is the one stated in Romans 12:1: "Therefore, I urge you, brothers, in view of God's mercy, to offer your bodies as living sacrifices, holy and pleasing to God—this is your spiritual act of worship."

You see, you already sacrificed everything when you accepted God's mercy! So don't go on about how many times you've tried to do this for yourself and failed. Instead, change your focus: this time, realize you are doing it for the Father! By building a strong mind and body that can serve God well, you are presenting an honorable sacrifice to God.

week 2
d a y 4

WHAT YOU EAT: Whole Grains

Let's start with the bottom of the food pyramid. The following diagram from the Pennsylvania Dietetic Association is helpful:[1]

The Pyramid Power Food Drive tells us to eat six to eleven servings of grain per day. Even when you consider that serving sizes are smaller than we tend to think, that may seem like a lot. However, nutritious grains should be 30–45 percent of a healthy person's diet. The key phrase here is *nutritious* grains.

Unfortunately, most of the grains Americans consume on a daily basis are closer to candies and sweets than they are to grains.

Why Whole Grains Are So Good

A diet of healthy grains is the basis of normal digestion. The right amount of dietary fiber and complex carbohydrates ensures proper bowel function, helps regulate cholesterol, and may lead to reduced risk of a number of diseases, such as colon cancer and Type II diabetes.

Whole grains are important because they are absorbed more slowly, which reduces the demand for insulin in the body. The high fiber acts as the body's lubricant to ensure the swift processing of foods, and this leads to fewer carbohydrates being absorbed and turning into sugar.

Pyramid Power Food Drive

Fats, Oils, & Sweets **Use Sparingly**			
	Jelly		
	Sugar		
	Syrup		
	Preserves		
	Vegetable oils		
	Light mayonnaise		
	Light salad dressings		

| Milk, Yogurt, & Cheese Group **2–3 Servings** | | Meat, Poultry, Fish, Dry Beans, Eggs, & Nuts Group **2–3 Servings** | |

Dried milk — Boxed milk — Infant formula — Canned yogurt — Evaporated milk — Boxed chocolate milk — Canned & boxed pudding — Carnation instant breakfast — Parmesan & romano cheese

Nuts — Beef stew — Bean soup — Baked beans — Canned chili — Peanut butter — Canned chicken — Dried beans & peas — Canned tuna or salmon

Vegetable Group 3–5 Servings

Tomato sauce — Tomato paste — Vegetable soup — Spaghetti sauce — Canned potatoes — Baby vegetables — Tomato & V8 juices — Instant mashed potatoes — Other canned vegetables

Raisins — Baby fruit — Applesauce — Fruit cocktail — Canned pumpkin — Other dried fruits — Canned & boxed 100% fruit juices — Canned pineapples — Canned pears, packed in juice — Other canned fruits, packed in juice

Fruit Group **2–4 Servings**

Bread, Cereal, Rice, & Pasta Group 6–11 Servings

Pancake mix — Rice pilaf — Rigatoni — Grits — Bread mix — White flour — Canned pasta soups

Brown rice — Spaghetti — Noodles — Canned pasta — Shredded wheat — Chicken noodle soup — Whole-grain crackers

Infant cereal — Macaroni — Oatmeal — Cold cereal — Cream of Wheat — Pretzels — Muffin mix

White rice — Cornmeal — Pasta, boxed — Graham crackers — Bran cereals — Whole-wheat flour — Macaroni & cheese mixes

Figure 3.

CHOOSE UNPROCESSED GRAINS

It's crucial from a nutritional and dietary standpoint to eat whole grains rather than processed grains.

If you do an analysis of refined flour, this is what you'll find:

◆ Almost 80 percent of the fiber has been removed.
◆ 20 percent of the protein has been removed.
◆ And over two-thirds (66 percent) of the B vitamins and minerals have been removed.

It is true that many flours are enriched. That is, they have vitamins that have been put back into the flour. However, these are usually artificially created, not vitamins from natural sources, so their total nutritional benefit is still questionable.

The process to refine flour removes the bran and germ—the main sources of fiber and minerals—from the plant, leaving the endosperm, or kernel, which is primarily carbohydrate. The minerals found in natural wheat are chelated (wrapped in protein). Chelation makes it much easier for the body to absorb these minerals. Most of the minerals replaced into fortified flour are not chelated.

To make matters worse, since the color of natural milled flour is not visually pleasing to the general consumer, the flour is bleached to give it its pure white color.

Natural grains are a testament to the miracle of God's creation. They should be the staple of your new healthy eating. You should replace processed forms of grain with as many natural grains as you can. Below is our first AWE Chart.

AWE: Grains, Breads, and Related Foods

avoid	watch	eat
Breads made with high amounts of fat oils, butter, etc. (e.g., fast food or canned biscuits)	White rice	Whole grains
	Bagels	Whole-grain brown rice
Nonenriched white flour	English muffins	Bran crackers
	Muffins	Whole-grain breads
Sugary breakfast cereals		Whole-grain breakfast cereals
Sweet breads		Pitas, tortillas, and other flat breads (especially whole grain)

Figure 4.

week 2
d a y 5

THE JOURNEY JOURNAL: Looking to the Future

Last week we talked about where you are. This week let's talk about where you want to be. Fill out the questions on the following page, and as you do, think about yourself in ten weeks' time—the wonderful new feelings, emotions, and hopes that await you at the end of this part of your journey.

WORKSHEET: Roadmap to Health

My weight-loss (improvement) goal per week (remember: one to two pounds is reasonable): _____

My total project weight-loss goal (improvement): _____

If I meet my goals, I will weigh: _____

Things I haven't done in a long time that I want to do again during this time: _____

_____

_____

_____

_____

Things I want to try to learn to like: _____

_____

_____

_____

_____

Types of foods I want to try I've never tried: _____

_____

_____

_____

_____

_____

_____

TAKE A WALK WITH GOD

Within the next twenty-four hours, take a "walk with God." Talk to Him about your hopes, your fears, and your dreams. Talk to Him about the help you need to reach your goals. Talk to Him as the Friend and Father He wants to be to you, and record your conversation in your journal.

week 2
d a y 6

MAKE IT REAL: A Success Graph

Remember: This is not the same old diet cycle you've tried in the past. You are running a race that has its finish line at the gates of heaven. It's a race for the rest of your life and a race for the quality of your life. However, I know that some of you won't be satisfied unless you are keeping some type of record.

One thing I don't like about normal weight-loss graphs is the emphasis on "loss." The graph itself shows a starting weight and then a line going down like the example below, even though illustrating great progress.

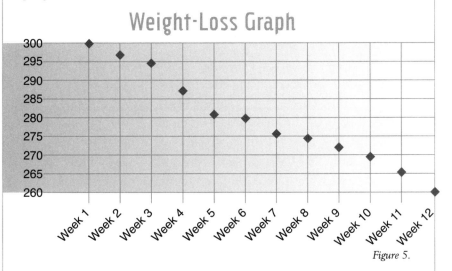

Figure 5.

We have been conditioned to think of graphs going downward as bad, probably because subconsciously we associate a downward trend with something negative, as in stock market and similar business graphs. Even the words *up* and *down* convey positive and negative emotions: "I'm feeling kind of down today," "Things are looking up," etc.

That's why I've designed something different—a success graph.

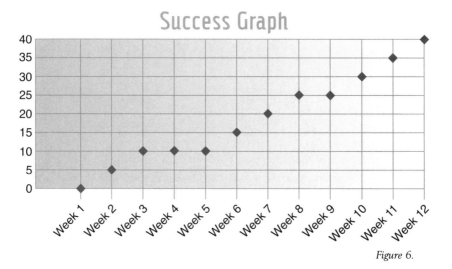

Figure 6.

A success graph charts pounds lost, so that when you lose weight, your chart is moving UP toward your goal. This might seem like a little thing, but it's important to diffuse any of the "mental mine fields" that can cause you to turn away from your goals.

If you're a chart kind of person, track your weight on the Success Graph (shown here and in appendix B) over the next twelve weeks. But, once again, keep in mind that the best feedback will come from your own body, as you begin to feel better and better. You will know you are losing weight without tracking it, but use the chart if it makes you feel better. However, do *not* weigh yourself more than once a week. Your weight can fluctuate three pounds or more in a given day, so establish a pattern of weighing yourself once a week, on the same day and near the same time, to get an idea of what your trend is.

You're also only going to work in twelve-week increments. As I said before, if you have a lot of weight to lose, you can feel defeated before you even get started if you are starting with a goal of forty, fifty, or even one hundred pounds. But remember, you only have to lose that next pound. It's one pound at a time, one baby step at a time. A mountain climber doesn't look at the mountain and try to figure out how to leap to the top. He looks for the best path up and *then* decides where to take that first step. And that's exactly what I'm encouraging you to do too. Winston Churchill's words remind us that nothing is impossible: "Every day you may make progress. Every step may be fruitful. Yet there will stretch out before you an ever-lengthening, ever-ascending, ever-improving path. You know you will never get to the end of the journey. But this, so far from discouraging, only adds to the joy and glory of the climb."

When Sir Churchill was prime minister of England, a lot more was on the line than just a cholesterol count! He led Britain through some of the darkest days of Europe's history. Yet far from being beaten and worn down by his task, he embraced it fully. That is the spirit we need to take forward with us.

week 2
d a y 7

A VOICE ALONG THE PATH: Kale's Story

So far so good. A few little slips here and there, but by and large, I've been eating better. The hardest part has been giving up what Dr. Jantz calls my "ritual eating." I've always tended to have a little snack at night before bedtime—popcorn, ice cream, etc. It was sort of my reward for getting through the day, my way of unwinding.

I always knew it wasn't a good idea to eat late at night, but I figured ice cream or popcorn wouldn't be that bad. Now I'm beginning to understand how bad that is on several different levels. From the physical side, snacks like that raise your insulin levels, which causes your body to store more fat. From the emotional side, it reinforces the idea that the day is an ordeal to get through, and food is the reward. The idea of taking my problems to God wasn't part of my thinking—I was too busy taking them to Ben & Jerry's.

Tonight, for the first time, I kept the snack down to an apple and substituted ice cream with a walk and a long talk with God. I missed my snack, but I seemed to sleep better.

I'm just beginning to realize how shallow my commitment has been at times. I guess it's time to learn to fill myself up with something besides food.

For encouragement along your path, visit www.aplaceofhope.com.

You were taught, with regard to your former way of life, to put off your old self, which is being corrupted by its deceitful desires; to be made new in the attitude of your minds; and to put on the new self, created to be like God in true righteousness and holiness.

—Ephesians 4:22–24

YOUR NEW BODY

week 3

d a y 1

INSPIRATION: A Makeover Mentality

It's time to tackle the body and body-image issue. It's no secret that in our society we associate beauty with goodness.

A special note to mothers and daughters: Visit http://www .waterhousepublications.com/index.htm and review the work of Debra Waterhouse, who specializes in body-image issues for moms and daughters.

Study after study shows that attractive people are more often given the benefit of the doubt, are more likely to be considered for that great job, etc. In short, we are a society attracted to attractive people! This preoccupation (some would say obsession) with physical beauty and body type has affected all Americans, but especially young females. This obsession is played out on television, in magazines, and in all forms of advertising. The Center treats hundreds of women every year for bulimia and anorexia. These women and girls didn't just wake up one morning and decide to try and starve themselves to death. It was a gradual response to Hollywood's perception of physical perfection—through not-so-subtle messages—bombarding them in the media.

The desire to be healthy—trim and fit—is right, proper and, I believe, a godly attribute. However, our society has taken this natural, normal desire and turned it into a soul poison—a desire to attain the unattainable perfection. And such images are thrown in our faces from every conceivable direction.

MISPERCEPTIONS

Sadly, we have even extended this "makeover" mentality to the image of our Savior. Look at the popular images different churches have of Jesus. Yes, different churches have different images of our Lord, since the skin tones of the portraits usually match those of the churchgoers, but there is a common theme—almost all depict a tall, attractive male with long hair.

But what does the Bible say? Build a mental picture in your mind of this man . . .

> He had no beauty or majesty to attract us to him, nothing in his appearance that we should desire him. He was despised and rejected by men, a man of sorrows, and familiar with suffering. Like one from whom men hide their faces he was despised, and we esteemed him not. Surely he took up our infirmities and carried our sorrows, yet we considered him stricken by God, smitten by him, and afflicted. But he was pierced for our trans-gressions, he was crushed for our iniquities; The punishment that brought us peace was upon him, and by his wounds we are healed. (Isaiah 53:2–5)

The aura surrounding Jesus does not come from His physical beauty. He was, in a word, unremarkable. Could God have chosen for Jesus to be beautiful? Of course! God could have given His Son beauty that would have shamed the angels. Why, then, did God choose for Jesus to be so plain?

We do not know the answer. We suspect, however, that it's the same reason Jesus was born to lowly parents. The same reason He was born in a little stall—not even a place meant for humans. Jesus came into this world in as humble a manner as you can imagine . . . and left by hanging on a cross as a common criminal.

But then the majesty and incredible awe of it—He rose as the master of all!

The Wonder of You

Take a moment tonight, before going to bed, to stand in front of a mirror. Look, *really* look, at your body for at least five minutes before filling out the worksheet at the end of this chapter. This time, rather than focusing on the potbelly or the cellulite or even a true physical deformity you may have, see the wonder there:

- Billions of cells constantly die and replenish at the rate of 25 million per second.
- In one square inch of skin, there are 4 yards of nerve fibers, 1300 nerve cells, 100 sweat glands, 3 million cells, and 3 yards of blood vessels.
- We see the world with new eyes each day. When we open our eyes the first time, the top layer of vision sensors are scorched away.
- Our ears can turn sound waves into electrochemical impulses through a canal system as beautiful and complex as a conch shell.
- The brain sends impulses racing between cells at 250 miles per hour.
- The heart beats 40 million times a year, sending blood cells on a hundred-mile journey to nourish your body through its 60,000-mile network of vessels.

But all these wonders pale when compared to the love and compassion of the human spirit. We have a wonderful capacity for goodness in a world that is sometimes dark and truly evil. Let me illustrate this with a story . . .

The Beauty of the Human Spirit

The year was 1941; the place was Auschwitz, Germany. Life in a German prison camp is something those who have not experienced it cannot imagine. The prisoners were systematically starved, worked to near death, and beaten. Among the thousands interred at Auschwitz is prisoner 16770, a polish priest named Maximilian Kolbe. At night, when most of the exhausted prisoners slept, Father

Kolbe would move from bunk to bunk, sharing with others a portion of the small meal he was given and offering prayers. He would give the prisoners what comfort he could and then urge them to pray for their captors.

In July 1941 a prisoner escaped from Kolbe's barracks. The standing order was that when one prisoner escaped, ten others would be sentenced to die by starvation—the most horrible form of execution the Nazis possessed. The morning after the escape, the prisoners were lined up and the ten were selected. Among these was Franciszek Gajowniczek, a young Polish man. Although it was forbidden for any prisoner to speak, Gajowniczek, overcome by grief, sobbed out ten words: "My poor wife, my poor children. What will they do?"

There was a movement among the assembled prisoners. To move out of formation meant a severe beating, but Father Kolbe quietly walked up to the front, removed his hat, and requested that he be allowed to die for Gajowniczek.

To speak to the commandant without permission was to invite immediate execution. Dumbfounded, the German commandant, Karl Fritsch, asked Kolbe to explain his request.

Kolbe replied, "I am a Catholic priest from Poland. I would like to take his place because I am old, and he has a wife and children."

Kolbe understood well that a healthy back was more valuable than an old man. Of course, none of us will ever know what thoughts the commandant had, but he agreed to the old man's request. Gajowniczek was returned to the ranks, and Father Kolbe was led away with the other nine to die.

Father Kolbe was thrown into Bunker 13 with the other nine condemned men. After two weeks the prisoners began to die, one by one. It was said that all during this time, Kolbe's prayers and encouragement could be heard. At the last only Father Kolbe was left. Since the cell was needed for new victims, on August 14, 1941, the Germans gave Kolbe an injection of carbolic acid, and he died, a prayer on his lips.

Franciszek Gajowniczek survived Auschwitz, and every year for the next five decades, he returned to Bunker 13 on August 14, paying homage to the man who had given up his life so that he could live. . . . [1]

I have thought often of this wonderful man's story. Father Kolbe, who called himself an "old man," was only forty-seven years of age. He was not handsome. Yet, without ever having met him, I am certain he was one of the more beautiful people to have walked this earth.

week 3
d a y 2

DEVOTIONAL: A Prayer of Thanks

WHAT'S ON YOUR FRIDGE?

> Sustain me according to your promise, and I
> will live; Do not let my hopes be dashed.
> (Psalm 119:116)

On a day-to-day basis, and especially when life can be discouraging, we sometimes forget what we have and what we are capable of achieving. But no matter how down or desperate your situation might be as you read these words, you wouldn't have to look far to find someone who is in a far worse situation, has far greater need, or who has faced far greater obstacles.

How important it is to be thankful for what you do have right now! Be thankful for the miracle of creation, thankful for the body and life you have, and thankful for this opportunity to improve yourself.

There is no greater prayer of thanks than Psalm 116. Let it be your prayer all throughout this week:

I love the LORD, for he heard my voice;
*   He heard my cry for mercy.*
Because he turned his ear to me,
*   I will call on him as long as I live.*

The cords of death entangled me,
  the anguish of the grave came upon me;
  I was overcome by trouble and sorrow.
Then I called on the name of the LORD; "O LORD, save me!"

The LORD is gracious and righteous;
  our God is full of compassion.
The LORD protects the simplehearted;
  when I was in great need, he saved me.

Be at rest once more, O my soul,
  for the LORD has been good to you.

For you, O LORD, have delivered my soul from death,
  my eyes from tears, my feet from stumbling,
that I may walk before the LORD
  in the land of the living.
I believed; therefore I said, "I am greatly afflicted."
And in my dismay I said, "All men are liars."

How can I repay the LORD for all his goodness to me?
I will lift up the cup of salvation
  and call on the name of the LORD.
I will fulfill my vows to the LORD
  in the presence of all his people.

Precious in the sight of the LORD is the death of his saints.
O LORD, truly I am your servant;
  I am your servant, the son of your maidservant;
  you have freed me from my chains.

I will sacrifice a thank offering to you
  and call on the name of the LORD.
I will fulfill my vows to the LORD in the presence of all his people,
in the courts of the house of the LORD—
  in your midst, O Jerusalem.

Praise the LORD.

week 3
d a y 3

THOUGHTS FOR FOOD: Glycemic Index and Glycemic Load

How many meals a day?

In 1999 researchers in Johannesburg, South Africa, did an interesting comparison study of large, infrequent meals versus smaller, more frequent meals.

They had two groups of healthy overweight men eat in two different methods. One group had a large breakfast, then nothing for five hours. The other group ate the same amount of food, but divided up so they ate the same portions every hour for five hours. Then both groups were allowed to have an all-you-can-eat lunch. On average, the group that ate the frequent, small meals reduced their appetite by 27 percent! Even more significant, the small-meal group had favorable insulin and blood-glucose profiles.[1]

To understand why this is, we need to consider how the body breaks down foods for energy.

UNDERSTANDING GLYCEMIC INDEX AND GLYCEMIC LOAD

All foods are broken down into sugars to be used by the body. When sugars are released into the body, the body reacts by producing insulin to reduce the sugar levels. Diseases like diabetes result when the body cannot produce enough insulin, or it builds up a resistance to insulin (which can lead to Type II diabetes). How much sugar (or glucose) goes into the bloodstream is measured by a scale called the Glycemic Index.

Traditionally, it was thought that foods high in sugars (like sodas, candy bars, etc.) caused sugar to enter the bloodstream the fastest. Surprisingly, studies have found that some carbohydrates actually release sugar into the bloodstream faster than common table sugar! As a way to compare how fast this release takes place in foods, a Glycemic Index has been set up to rank carbohydrates' immediate effect on blood glucose. The higher the number, the faster the blood glucose response; therefore, foods with a high number should be avoided. In general, a Glycemic Index (GI) of 70 or more is considered high, while a GI of less than 55 is considered low.

After reading the section on grains and processed foods in the last chapter, you are probably not surprised to learn that sugar and white bread have a high GI of 100. However, looking at the Glycemic Index alone is not a good indicator of which foods to avoid. For example, cereals made from cornflakes coated with sugar have a GI of 55, while cereals such as Grape Nuts have a GI of 67! This might lead you to conclude that you should forego the "healthy" cereals and load up on the sugared ones. For another example, a raw carrot has a GI almost as high as pure glucose. However, we all know that carrots do not have the same effect on the body that eating raw sugar would.

Researchers have recently realized that the GI only tells part of the story. It not only matters how fast a sugar is introduced into your bloodstream, but also how much is introduced in a normal serving. For this reason, researchers developed a measure called the Glycemic Load (GL). The GL multiplies the GI by the amount of carbohydrates a food contains. The GL gives a much more accurate measure of how a food is going to affect your blood-sugar levels.

It's important to consider not only the Glycemic Index but also the Glycemic Load. You'll find a chart listing some common foods and their Glycemic Load measurement in appendix C.

For a more complete list, visit www.glycemicindex.net. This is a Web site of the University of Sydney in Australia. By clicking on the GI Database option on the menu, on the left side, you will be able to enter the name of a particular food, such as banana. When I did this, it produced a list of different types of banana and banana products. Click on the individual item, and even more information becomes available. Use this information as a supplemental guide when choosing the types of foods you wish to add or delete from your diet.

CHANGE YOUR HABITS!

New Habit #3: Eat smaller and more frequent meals.

Processing large amounts of calories at one sitting creates a massive glucose dump into your system that causes your body to counteract with a surge of insulin. This surge can cause an insulin excess, making you feel hungry and shaky. This is the kind of glucose-insulin roller coaster you want to avoid! Eat less, but more often. Turn that roller coaster into a gentle, consistent wave of moderation.

week 3
d a y 4

WHAT YOU EAT: Processed or Unprocessed?

There is a growing feeling among health professionals that, after our poor eating habits, the next biggest culprit for the growing obesity and dietary-related illnesses in America might be the ever-increasing amount of processed foods we eat.

Processed foods include foods such as white flour, hydrogenated cooking oils, or any food that undergoes extensive processing before getting to the consumer.

Let's consider one of the foods we've already discussed at the base of the pyramid—grains. The typical flour you have in your cupboard is not whole grain; it is the endosperm (the kernel) of the wheat. The endosperm is essentially pure starch. Most of the healthy components of wheat—the dietary fiber, the B vitamins, etc.—are contained in the bran and the husk. These are removed during processing, and the wheat kernels are ground and bleached to produce white flour. This pattern is consistent with all heavily processed foods—the steps taken to make them ready for the average consumer actually rob the consumer of most of the benefits of the food!

Another example of the effects of processing is cooking oils. Many cooking oils are hydrogenated or partially hydrogenated oils. This means the oil is heated to a high temperature and then treated with hydrogen gas to increase the shelf life. According to a notice on the American Heart Association Web site:

> In clinical studies, trans-fatty acids or hydrogenated fats tend to raise total blood cholesterol levels, but less than more saturated fatty acids. Trans-fatty acids also tend to raise LDL ("bad") cholesterol and lower HDL ("good") cholesterol when used instead of cis fatty acids or natural oils. These changes may increase the risk of heart disease.[2]

There is mounting evidence that many of our modern methods of processing foods contribute to a host of chronic illnesses.

So what's the solution?

CHOOSE UNPROCESSED FOODS OVER PROCESSED

Using foods as close to their natural state as possible means using them as God placed them on the earth. It seems that time and again we have to learn what incredible wonders of balance and purpose lie in such simple things as a stalk of natural wheat.

week 3
d a y 5

THE JOURNEY JOURNAL: Take a Good Look!

Spend a full five minutes examining your body in the mirror. Then fill out the worksheet on the following page.

WORKSHEET: What Did I See?

*What one thing do I most dislike about my body, and why?*_____

_____

_____

_____

_____

_____

Do I have the power to change that thing? Why or why not? _____

_____

_____

_____

If so, how? _____

_____

_____

Name at least three things you like about your body. _____

_____

_____

_____

_____

What can you do today to enhance the positives about your body? ____

_____

_____

_____

_____

You're a Miracle!

After you've completed the worksheet, reread day 1—especially the part that details some of the wonders of the human body. Close your eyes and visualize the wonders taking place inside your body right now.

After a minute or two, open your eyes. Look at your body again. Do you see yourself in a different light?

Share your thoughts on this exercise in your personal journal.

week 3
d a y 6

MAKE IT REAL: Hit the Bull's-Eye!

Over the next few weeks, I'd like you to keep track of where you are in meeting some basic daily goals. On the sample "bull's-eye" (see figure 8 on page 59) are four important, easy-to-track goals.

At the top is "Ate a healthy breakfast." I want you to be successful from the very start of your day!

The second is "Drank 64 oz. of water." Remember, water is the most important food you can give your body. Start early and continue to drink throughout the day.

The third is "Ate high-fiber foods." These are the healthy, whole-grain choices that will fill you up and give you the nutrition you need to meet the day.

The fourth is "Avoided high-fat foods." I put this last because often we start the day resolute in our desire to do the right thing. By the time afternoon and evening roll around, however, that desire can be overshadowed by our habits, including evening eating and snacking on high-fat foods.

Each week, using the Did I Meet My Goals? chart (figure 7 on page 58), grade yourself from one to five (one being good, five being bad) on how you did in meeting your four eating habit goals. Mark the appropriate number for each goal, and draw a line between them (see appendix D for your own Hit the Bull's-Eye!). The goal is to move closer to the bull's-eye every week, as shown in the Sample Bull's-Eye, figure 8. Keep your goals consistent and positive through the day and evening, and over time you should see your marks spiraling in toward the center.

Did I Meet My Goals?				
Aim	Ate a healthy breakfast	Drank 64 oz. of water	Ate high-fiber foods	Avoided high-fat foods
1	Ate every day this week	Drank 64 oz. every day	Ate high-fiber foods every day	Ate foods with less than 30% fat every day
2	Ate most days this week	Drank 64 oz. most days	Ate high-fiber foods most days	Ate foods with less than 30% fat most days
3	Ate half the days this week	Drank 64 oz. half the days	Ate high-fiber foods half the days	Ate foods with less than 30% fat half the days
4	Ate some days this week	Drank 64 oz. some days	Ate high-fiber foods some of the days	Ate foods with less than 30% fat some of the days
5	Do Pop-Tarts count?	Had a Big Gulp with my donuts	Do Pop-Tarts count?	Krispy Kreme just gave me my own parking spot.

Figure 7.

Sample Bull's-Eye

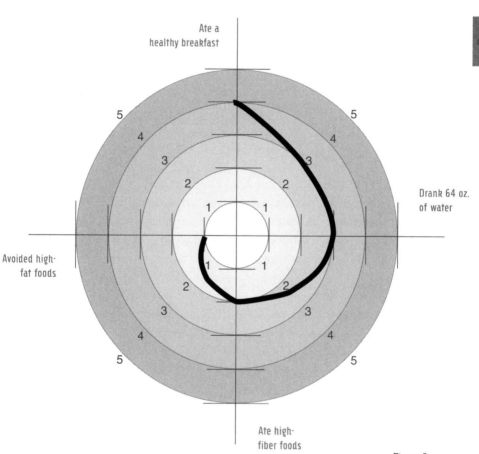

Ate a
healthy breakfast

Drank 64 oz.
of water

Avoided high-
fat foods

Ate high-
fiber foods

Figure 8.

week 3
d a y 7

A VOICE ALONG THE PATH: Kale's Story

I didn't like standing in front of the mirror at all.

That five minutes felt more like five years. I have to admit, however, after the first minute or so of verbal personal insults, I finally decided to try and really do as the exercise intended. No, I'm not a TV star, but I'm not ugly either. I have nice eyes. I have a nice smile.

I have hands that can hold the hand of someone hurting. I have arms that can give someone a hug when they need it. I have a voice that can be used to call someone who is lonely.

In other words, I am an instrument of God. He put me here to do His work, and I'm afraid I haven't treated His instrument very well.

But, just like a vintage auto that has been neglected, the potential is still there. Sure, I need a little "body work" and some cleaning, but I can be better, healthier, than I was ten, even fifteen years ago. I can be in mint condition again.

And I can be a better instrument for God.

So built we the wall; and all the wall was joined together unto the half thereof: for the people had a mind to work.

—Nehemiah 4:6 KJV

YOUR NEW MIND

week 4

d a y 1

INSPIRATION: The Problem of Overeating

The first part of any good reconstruction involves the tearing down of the old to make way for the new. Hopefully by this point we have managed to clear the land, so to speak. That means feelings of inadequacy must go. They are useless and get us nowhere. We are *all* inadequate compared to God, and yet, if we choose, we can be accepted into His family. But we are accepted by grace—not by any physical, mental, or emotional value we may think others (or we ourselves) possess.

Instead of generating feelings of disappointment, dissatisfaction, and despair that inevitably come when you compare yourself with others (as we mentioned in the last chapter), focus on only one thing: how do you feel today compared with how you felt in the beginning of this program?

Do you feel better?

Do you have more energy?

Are you able to do more and more during your activities?

Those are the only comparisons that matter.

In this chapter we'll explore how you can turn your mind away from thoughts of overeating and self-defeat . . . and in doing so turn your mind more toward God, who values you, even when you are inadequate: "God demonstrates his own love for us in this: While we were still sinners, Christ died for us" (Romans 5:8).

Here are some words from the apostle Paul to help shape our thoughts: "Whatever is true, whatever is noble, whatever is right, whatever is pure, whatever is lovely, whatever is admirable—if anything is excellent or praiseworthy—think about such things" (Philippians 4:8).

WHY DO WE OVEREAT?

The human mind is a wondrous creation, an amazing tool with the power to inspire us to victory or to overwhelm us with defeat. Targeted below are some of the reasons we use for overeating, as well as ways we can turn the tool of the mind to a more constructive purpose.

Reason #1: We eat to reward ourselves.

Sometimes, when the world is treating us especially rough, we feel that we owe ourselves a little treat, to spoil ourselves a little bit with the infamous comfort foods. Because foods like chocolate cause a release of endorphins into the body, eating certain foods really *does* make you feel better . . . at least for a time. However, like any chemically induced solution, it is only temporary. As your bad feelings about your weight compounds the likelihood you will suffer "down" moments, you can quickly find yourself in an eat-and-regret spiral that leads to more and more weight gains.

If you're concerned that there may be a strong emotional/physical link to your overeating, you'll find the quiz in week 4, day 6, especially eye opening.

Instead of rewarding yourself by feeding your body, reward yourself by feeding your mind. Enjoy a favorite activity, go to a movie (but no buttery popcorn!), or take a walk with God and talk your problems over with Him. Read an inspirational book, spend some time with your family, or tackle some little item around the house that for a long time has been on your "I have to fix that" list. The sense of accomplishment will help offset the down mood you were in.

Here's a little perspective: No matter what kind of day we have, we will never come close to experiencing what Jesus did His last week on earth. What wrongs have we suffered that can compare to His? What pain have we felt that measures up? What humiliation could possibly compare with that walk through Jerusalem up to the Place of Skulls? There is none. Yet knowing that Jesus, who suffered far beyond what we will ever go through, is up in heaven encouraging us onward is true encouragement indeed.

Reason #2: We eat to punish ourselves.

"No one else cares about me, so why should I care about myself? I'm having a donut!"

This is really a variation on the "reward" trap. Although we recognize the bad effects of overeating; feelings of inadequacy, low self-esteem, etc., have us believing that we don't deserve any better.

Instead of focusing on how you value yourself, focus on how much God values you. "Are not five sparrows sold for two pennies? Yet not one of them is forgotten by God. Indeed, the very hairs of your head are all numbered. Don't be afraid; you are worth more than many sparrows" (Luke 12:6–7).

God never looks at us and sees the failures, disappointments, or shortcomings. He looks at us and sees the good that is in us and the greatness that could be and loves us. When you can't believe in your own worth, focus on the worth you are in God's eyes and repay that love by respecting His creation.

Reason #3: We eat as a defense mechanism.

If you are overweight and unattractive, then you won't have to deal with the uncertainty of relationships. You'll know where you stand. This attitude is common among people who have been overweight and have some success losing weight. When friends and associates start to notice, it can make the person who is losing weight uncomfortable.

When someone remarks on how much you've lost, don't say things like "Still a long way to go" or "Not as much as I should have lost." Instead, embrace these compliments as affirmation of the transformation you have chosen! Tell them, "You ain't seen nothin' yet!"

Reason #4: We eat when we are bored.

It's amazing that, with all the time demands we have in our lives, we still get bored. To relieve the feeling of restlessness, we often resort to eating.

If this is your problem, fill out the first column of the Action Sheet on the next page. You can fill in activities like "read a book," "go for a walk," "call a friend," or "go shopping." Then the next time you feel like eating, take your Action Sheet and choose an activity that you can do to replace or postpone eating. Next to that activity, in the second column, write the food you want to eat and the date. Then, go do the activity you've chosen, and come back to your sheet to complete the third column. What was the outcome? Maybe you chose not to eat that cookie at all. Maybe you decided to go ahead and eat the cookie, but you did it purposefully or because of hunger, and not out of boredom. Finally, assess your feelings about your decision. You might write "It was worth it!" or "It wasn't worth it" or "It felt great to say no!" or "I wasn't hungry."

Reason #5: We fill ourselves full, because we aren't fulfilled.

Read those words again since it's a big idea to get our minds around. Many of us feel an empty place inside. The cause can be varied—lack of a partner to share our lives, loss of a loved one, depression due to life situations, or other circumstances. Many times we try to fill that empty place with food—and, of course, it just doesn't work.

If you have any reason to suspect the cause is a real medical condition, then get your body checked out as soon as possible. Depression can have real physical causes, so if you're suffering from this, see a doctor . . . for your own peace of mind if nothing else!

Fulfillment is not achieved through accomplishments or "success." How many successful people admit they struggle with addiction, marital conflict, even thoughts of suicide? Just check out the magazine headlines in the grocery store for evidence that worldly success doesn't bring immunity from troubles!

So where does fulfillment really come from?

Fulfillment comes from diving in and acting upon the will of God. Has God been speaking to your heart, asking you to act on something? God has a plan for you, a purpose and a mission for your life, a means to utilize your talents and abilities to further His kingdom— in short, a God-given destiny! That doesn't mean you have to run off and be a missionary—God's plan involves those who work in the average office as much as those who carry His word to the distant

Action Sheet		
Activities that replace or postpone eating	Desired food	Outcome and assessment
	date_____	
	date_____	
	date_____	
	date_____	
	date_____	

Figure 9.

parts of this planet. Have you been open to His plan, His calling that has been placed on your heart? Or have you been trying to bend God's desires to fit in with your own earthly goals? It's time to take an honest assessment of where you are, no matter how much or how little success you have had, and make sure that your journey and God's path for you are the same. Think about what God wants for you, and write your thoughts in your journal.

week 4

d a y 2

DEVOTIONAL: Doing God's Will

WHAT'S ON YOUR FRIDGE?

> Not everyone who says to me, "Lord, Lord," will
> enter the kingdom of heaven, but only he who
> does the will of my Father who is in heaven.
> (Matthew 7:21)

Are you open to knowing—and then doing—God's will?

Often we treat God like an answering machine. We scurry around in our busy lives. Then when we get a moment of quiet, we sit down, hit the playback button, and expect God to recite off His plan for us. (We hope He will be brief and to the point, so we can get back to what we were doing.)

We want a convenience-store God, a drive-thru God, a while-u-wait God.

We want God to appreciate just how *busy* we are and work within *our* schedules. I'm certain that at times God smiles down on us in amusement at our own self-importance. Like Job, we sometimes forget just who and what God is.

Commit yourself to living His agenda this week, not yours. Make it a point to be listening with your heart for His voice—not just when you can fit it in, but every waking moment. Make it your prayer this week to be open to His plans for you.

Heavenly Father,

How much this world can draw me in! I often strain so hard to fill every moment and every second with some purpose, some meaning, that I forget that You are my purpose and my meaning. Create in me a clean heart this week, and renew a right spirit within me. Make me open to Your will and let me hear Your voice, and provide me with the strength and resolve to do that which You would have me do. Help me as I strive to improve myself and my body so that I might be a better servant. Amen.

week 4
d a y 3

THOUGHTS FOR FOOD: Food Combinations

I've already talked a lot about processed versus nonprocessed food and about how certain foods raise your blood sugar. This week I'll explain more how this affects weight loss and the ways in which different food combinations can accelerate healthy weight loss.

CHANGE YOUR HABITS!

New Habit #4: Think about food combinations.

In our discussions about how foods are absorbed into the body, I haven't yet talked about the role eating plays in basic digestion. Different foods are digested in different ways. For example, starches are primarily digested by alkaline substances (specifically, ptyalin in your saliva). Proteins, such as meat, digest most effectively in an acid solution (i.e., the hydrochloric acid contained in your stomach).

Unfortunately, basic chemistry teaches us that alkalis and acids tend to cancel each other out, which reduces the effectiveness of digestion.

Food combinations are not something to obsess over. Your diet needs to contain a healthy balance of all the food groups at all times, because you are establishing eating habits that will continue for the rest of your life, not just for the course of this program.

However, an awareness of which food combinations work well in digestion can be useful in meal planning, so we've included a simple diagram below. Especially if you decide to follow the idea of smaller, more frequent meals, this diagram can help in choosing food combinations. Our goal is to give you tools that let you run your "engine" as efficiently as possible. An efficient system equates to a higher and healthier metabolism.

Food Combinations

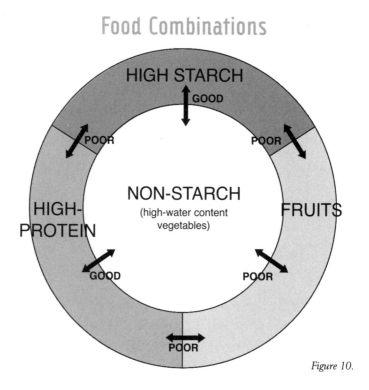

Figure 10.

You can see that nonstarch vegetables high in water content (green beans, lettuce, etc.) combine well with proteins and starches. Note that most other food combinations work against each other. Does this mean you should never have meat and potatoes together again? Of course not! We also know that some lifestyles don't lend themselves to having a small meal every hour. As with all the recommendations I make in this book, these are guidelines to help you make sound eating decisions today and every day for the rest of your life.

week 4
d a y 4

WHAT YOU EAT: Fruits

In this section I'll tackle the next level of the food pyramid, starting with the fruit group.

CRAVING A SWEET SNACK?

Fruits are pure carbohydrates, and as we all know, fruits are sweet. This might make it sound as if fruits should be avoided by anyone trying to lose weight. As we have alluded to before, however, different foods affect the body differently, and the same is true for fruit.

Let's take a look at the GI and GL numbers for some common fruits. (Note that the GLs are calculated by taking each fruit's Glycemic Index and multiplying it by the USDA figures for the number of carbohydrates in a normal serving.)

Fruit GI/GL					
Fruit	Glycemic Index	Glycemic Load	Fruit	Glycemic Index	Glycemic Load
Apple	38	6	Orange	42	5
Banana	51	13	Raisins	64	28
Grapefruit	25	3	Tomato	38	4
Grapes	46	8	Watermelon	72	4

Figure 11.

As you can see, GI and GL give very different pictures with some fruits. For example, watermelons have a high GI of 72, but they have a low GL of 4. This is because watermelon contains relatively few carbohydrates in a normal serving. Raisins have a lower GI of 64, but because they are a dried fruit, the sugar concentration is very high in a normal serving. Therefore, they get a very high GL of 28. (A GL of 1–10 is considered low, 11–19 is medium, and 20 and above is high.)

Fruits are a wonderful source of nutrients and, along with vegetables, are some of the best antioxidant foods you can eat. There is clinical evidence that some fruits, such as apples, can lower LDL (bad) cholesterol levels and suppress appetite. Fruits also help to regulate digestion and ensure normal bowel function.

A selection of low GL fruits is an important component of your new healthy eating habits. When craving a sweet snack, fruits with low GL should be the first option.

AWE: Fruits

avoid	watch	eat
Dates, figs, raisins (high GL value)	Bananas	Melons
Avocados	Orange juice	Apples
	Any juices with sweeteners added and/or pulp removed	Most other fruits have a good GL rating (check the chart in appendix C to be sure)

Figure 12.

week 4
d a y 5

THE JOURNEY JOURNAL: Emotional Eating

Is there a strong emotional basis for your overeating? The following self-test will help you find out.

WORKSHEET: How Emotionally Tied Am I to My Food?

- ☐ I grew up as a perfectionist.
- ☐ My father had high expectations, whether verbalized or not.
- ☐ I am firstborn.
- ☐ My mother has a history of dieting.
- ☐ A lot of focus was placed on weight and appearance in my family.
- ☐ I grew up in a home where my father was emotionally distant.
- ☐ I had a high desire to please my father.
- ☐ I attempted to gain my father's approval.
- ☐ My mother was codependent.
- ☐ My father was an addict.
- ☐ I grew up in a home with very strict discipline (overly so), where punishment was severe and physical.
- ☐ My parents used guilt/shame as a method to discipline or punish.
- ☐ Sexuality was either not discussed at all or treated in a "dirty" manner.
- ☐ If I'm a daughter, my father complained to me about my mother.
- ☐ I was forced to be an adult, even when I was a child.
- ☐ As a daughter, I "raised" other siblings.
- ☐ I was not allowed to be "just a kid."
- ☐ I have been sexually abused.
- ☐ I have been fondled . . . or more.
- ☐ I have experienced incest.

I have been a victim of:

- ❏ neglect
- ❏ verbal abuse

I have one or more of these biochemical imbalances:

- ❏ brain allergies
- ❏ hypoglycemia
- ❏ PMS

I have an addiction to diets and dieting in one of the following areas:

- ❏ compulsive dieting
- ❏ fasting
- ❏ diuretic use
- ❏ laxative abuse
- ❏ prescription drug abuse
- ❏ I have a desire to over-please (I over-control through people pleasing).
- ❏ I tend to ignore or deny anger.
- ❏ I overuse food for pleasure or reward.
- ❏ Food becomes the main focus for pleasure.

Did you recognize yourself in even one of the self-test items? If so, your eating may be tied to your emotions. Sometimes professional support may be necessary to help you deal with the issues that cause you to overeat. Spend some time in your journal writing about any emotional ties to food you may have and what the reasons may be.

week 4

d a y 6

MAKE IT REAL: Exercise

It's time to get to everyone's absolute favorite topic: exercise.

You knew we'd get around to it sooner or later, right? It's time to start thinking about adding exercise to your new lifestyle.

The benefits of exercise have been documented so often that it hardly seems necessary to go into the reasons. But for motivation, here are some of the biggest ones:

- ◆ Exercise promotes weight loss not only by burning calories but by increasing the body's metabolic rate. The fat-burning benefits of exercise last well beyond the time you are exercising.

- ◆ Exercise improves your mood and sense of well-being, because the physical exertion releases the "feel good" endorphins into your body.

- ◆ Lack of exercise can kill. According to the American Heart Association, 250,000 deaths per year in the U.S. can be attributed to a lack of exercise. In addition, a study published in the *New England Journal of Medicine* determined that being overweight and/or obese may account for 90,000 U.S. cancer deaths per year.

There is no avoiding it—exercise is necessary for your long-term health. It's time to make it a priority in your life and in your daily routine.

WHAT TYPE OF EXERCISE?

That answer is simple: the type you will do. A relatively "poor" exercise that you will do on a regular basis is much better than a wonderful exercise you do once every two weeks or less.

One exercise that's easy to incorporate is walking. So why not commit to a regular walking routine? Remember that Jesus walked thousands of miles in His life. Based on His travels recorded in the Bible, it's estimated that during His three-year ministry alone, Jesus walked more than 3,000 miles!

Plan on taking a walk with God every evening—for a half hour if you can. Use this time to discuss your day, your thoughts, and your feelings. Also explore His purpose for you and be open to His will. Those benefits far outweigh even the positive health aspects.

Exercise comes in many shapes and forms. There are a lot of opportunities for "mini" workouts during the course of your day.

Look over the checklist below, and commit to doing some of these easy-to-incorporate exercises every chance you get during the week and for the rest of the program.

EASY-TO-INCORPORATE EXERCISES

- ◆ When you go shopping, park as far away from the store as you safely can. Then walk.
- ◆ Turn housework into a game. Shoot baskets with the laundry at the washer, do some knee bends as you sweep or vacuum the floor, etc.
- ◆ If you do lawn work, do a little extra with the push mower instead of the riding mower. Even a couple of trips around the lawn before hopping on the tractor can make a difference.
- ◆ Incorporate exercise into your TV time. "Buy" your TV time with some sit-ups, leg lifts, etc. Set up your walking machine near the TV, and do a light walk during your favorite thirty-minute program.

- ◆ Don't drive to visit your neighbor down the road or to get milk from a nearby store. Leave the car keys in your pocket and walk.
- ◆ When was the last time you played ball with your kids (who cares if they're thirty years old) or with friends?

In your journal or binder, write down a series of activities that you used to enjoy but gave up for some reason or another. Then write down some activities you've always contemplated doing but have never tried. Make a commitment during this program to do at least one thing from each of these two lists every week.

week 4

d a y 7

A VOICE ALONG THE PATH: Kale's Story

Well, I blew up today.

I was talking to Dr. Jantz about how I should be eating, and he kept pointing back to the guidelines we have covered so far. I listened for a while, but finally I just threw up my hands.

"Dr. Jantz, we are three weeks into this program, and you haven't given me a diet plan. We've only talked about a few of the foods I eat. I'm never going to lose much weight in these twelve weeks unless we get on with it!"

Dr. J just smiled calmly. (I hate it when people are being calm when I'm going off the edge!) "Kale, you may not lose a great deal of weight in these twelve weeks."

I began to argue. "But then why set all those goals? Why—"

Dr. J held up his hand. "I said you might not. You've already started to change your eating habits—reducing your portions, substituting more frequent, smaller meals. You have also started walking regularly. And you have lost some weight."

"Some," I admitted. "But I'm not on track to hit my goal."

"One of the problems with typical diet plans," he explained, "is that they try and hurry you into the diet so you can start seeing results right away. Well, if a program is intended to last only twelve weeks, then it makes sense to hurry into it, I suppose. But we're

establishing habits you'll want to carry with you for the next forty, fifty, who knows how many years. When you think of it in those terms, it's important to take the time to put each piece of the puzzle into place. To not rush on to something else until you have firmly established each new change in your lifestyle. The next nine weeks won't determine the success of your program—the next ten years will."

"Maybe," I said doubtfully. "But I'd feel a lot better if I was seeing some dramatic results."

"I know." Dr. J smiled again. "But, sadly, most of the people who have had dramatic results have had just as dramatic relapses. There really aren't any quick fixes, not if you're doing this for life."

Well, I am doing this for life and for the quality of my life. I guess I'm just as much of a quick-fix junkie as everyone else. Even though I know what he's saying is right, I still wish a magic wand could fix me right now.

I guess God and I have a lot to talk about on our walk tonight.

the total temple makeover

If anyone is in Christ, he is a new creation; the old has gone, the new has come!

—2 Corinthians 5:17

YOUR NEW SPIRIT

week 5

d a y 1

INSPIRATION: A New Spirit

You cannot be the person you were, because the person you were was overweight. Learning to become healthy and active is like learning to be a child of God—you don't grow up all at once. Peter expressed the need for rebirth beautifully: "Therefore, rid yourselves of all malice and all deceit, hypocrisy, envy, and slander of every kind. Like newborn babies, crave pure spiritual milk, so that by it you may grow up in your salvation, now that you have tasted that the Lord is good" (1 Peter 2:1–2).

By now you should be at the "toddler" stage. You should be seeing the changes that are going on in your body, and you should be feeling better at this stage, if you have followed the path laid out so far.

This week we'll explore how to create a new spirit within—one that will help you live your remaining days in health and happiness.

As you work on your physical being, make sure you don't neglect your spiritual being. However, we don't grow spiritually all at once any more than we lose the weight we need to lose all at once. We grow in spirit by reading God's Word, meeting with other Christians, and seeking out those who can teach us more about being a Christian.

All the clients who have come through the Center have started out being fixated on their bodies. In almost all cases, they regret later that they didn't realize an important connection: if they had attended to their spiritual health as well as their physical health, success would have been easier to achieve. For it is within your *spiritual* self that the true miracles of transformation await you: "For God did not give us a spirit of timidity, but a spirit of power, of love and of self-discipline" (2 Timothy 1:7).

week 5
d a y 2

DEVOTIONAL: Create in Me a Pure Heart
WHAT'S ON YOUR FRIDGE?

> Create in me a pure heart, O God, and renew a
> steadfast spirit within me. (Psalm 51:10)

The songs of David reveal a man who knows more than his share of troubles, who stumbled more than a few times in his walk with God. They also reveal a man who deeply desired to know and do the will of his Creator. Therefore, let's use these words from Psalm 143:7–11 this week as our prayer, to ask the Lord to comfort us, to lift us up, and to fill us with His spirit.

> *Answer me quickly, O LORD; my spirit fails. Do not hide your face from me or I will be like those who go down to the pit. Let the morning bring me word of your unfailing love, for I have put my trust in you. Show me the way I should go, for to you I lift up my soul. Rescue me from my enemies, O LORD, for I hide myself in you. Teach me to do your will, for you are my God; may your good Spirit lead me on level ground.*

week 5
d a y 3

THOUGHTS FOR FOOD: Healthy Meal Planning

Just as there are some simple guidelines for choosing foods, there are simple general guidelines for preparing food to help you gain the most benefits.

CHANGE YOUR HABITS!

New Habit #5: Think about fresh, low-fat ways to prepare food.

The following are some helpful ideas to incorporate your new habit when preparing food:

- Use minimal oil. When frying foods, use the least oil possible. When a dish allows it, use monounsaturated oils, such as olive oil and canola oil. Without a doubt, extra-virgin olive oil should be your first choice, as it has NO saturated fats and is pressed, not processed. Avoid oils high in saturated fats, such as butter and shortening.
- Always use ingredients that are as fresh and natural as possible. Review the recommendations for each type of food group you are using in your cooking.
- Substitute low-fat alternatives when possible. Use skim milk

in place of whole milk and low-fat yogurt in place of cream and low-fat or fat-free varieties of sour cream.

◆ Remove skin and large sections of fat from meats before preparation.

◆ Don't overcook foods. This will rob them of vital nutrients.

◆ Baking, broiling, and steaming are better choices than deep frying, pan frying, or grilling. In general, go with cooking methods that don't require oil.

◆ Use low-fat methods of seasoning your food—lemon juice, fresh herbs, salsa, etc.

◆ Use low-fat condiments, such as mustard, horseradish, and picante, rather than mayo and butter. (If you simply *have* to have butter, try mixing 3 parts butter with 1 part olive oil and a few herbs of your choice and use sparingly. This helps reduce the saturated-fat levels and increases the proportion of poly- and monounsaturated fats.) Use a nonfat or low-fat ranch dressing on potatoes, rather than butter and sour cream.

Healthy meal planning is a learning process. However, everyone can prepare meals that they and their families will enjoy—meals that will satisfy their hunger and help improve their overall health.

week 5
d a y 4

WHAT YOU EAT: Vegetables

The next food group to discuss is—you guessed it—vegetables! But are all vegetables created equal? Are they always healthy?

Remember what we learned about fruits and Glycemic Loads in chapter 4? Well, vegetables have Glycemic Loads too. In general, starchy vegetables (particularly potatoes) carry a high GL. Look over figure 13 on the next page.

Potatoes should not be a staple of a healthy diet, as they carry both a high GI and GL. However, they are the most consumed vegetable in the U.S. In fact, after milk products, potatoes are the most consumed food, with studies showing that the average American ate 138 pounds of potatoes in 1999! What makes it even worse, of course, is that the bulk of these potatoes are consumed as French fries and potato chips, after having been deep fried in hydrogenated oils, literally bathed in trans-fats.

It's not a coincidence that overweight people tend to be starch junkies. If you fall into that category, you need to wean yourself away from having potatoes as a large portion of your diet. That doesn't mean you can never have a potato again, but be aware of the effects on your insulin levels. A healthier choice would be vegetable-based soups, as well as juices, such as V-8. These, along with corn, peas, carrots, salads, and similar vegetables, can provide a valuable substitute for potatoes. Also onions, peppers, chilies, and other spicy vegetables can add a nice zest to a lot of different dishes without adding a lot of salt, butter, or other seasonings.

GI/GL of Vegetables

Item	GI	GL	Grams Per Serving
Broad beans	79	9	80
Green peas	48	3	80
Pumpkin	75	3	80
Sweet corn	54	9	80
Beet root	64	5	80
Carrots	47	3	80
Cassava, boiled	46	12	100
Parsnips	97	12	80
Baked potato	85	26	150
Desiree potato, boiled	101	17	150
White potato, cooked	50	14	150
French fries	75	22	150
Instant mashed potatoes	85	17	150
New potato	57	12	150
Sweet potato	61	17	150

Figure 13.

AWE: Vegetables

avoid	watch	eat
Starchy vegetables (Potatoes) Deep-fried vegetables	Sweet potatoes	Green vegetables Carrots Most nonstarchy vegetables

Figure 14.

week 5
d a y 5

THE JOURNEY JOURNAL: A Recipe Hunt

Instead of filling out a worksheet this week, we'll go on a recipe hunt. We'll start with recipes that will reduce your potato consumption. Using the Internet, local library, a friend's recipes, and so on, find five to ten vegetable dishes this week that you can substitute for potatoes. Paste or record them in your journal and make a commitment to try them all during the next two weeks. Try one or two new dishes a week to shift your eating to new and better meals.

If you own a palm-based PDA device, there is an excellent resource on the Web: go to http://diabetestype2.ca/glycemic/ and download their palm database of GL foods. This will give you a list to take with you when you grocery shop or when you sit down to make out a shopping list.

Green, nonstarchy vegetables, in general, are a great low GL food. As you can see from the chart in day 4 of this week, most green vegetables have a GL value below 20, and many have a GL value below 10. For quick, light snacks, turn to nonstarchy vegetables.

It's no secret that Americans don't eat enough vegetables, so start making the change in your diet. The following is a good recipe to get you started. Portobello mushrooms aren't cheap, but they make a sandwich that could almost make you forget burgers. Here is a quick and easy way to fix them.

Portobello Burger

Ingredients
1 tablespoon olive oil
1 large Portobello mushroom, stem removed
sprinkle garlic salt
couple splashes Worcestershire sauce
sprig parsley, cut up
1 slice Swiss cheese
1 whole-grain hamburger bun

Instructions
1. Heat oil in skillet on medium-high heat for one minute.
2. Lay mushroom in pan and sprinkle with garlic salt, Worcestershire sauce, and parsley.
3. Cook two minutes on each side, or until lightly browned.
4. Cover pan, lower heat to medium, and cook five minutes.
5. Place cheese over mushroom. Cover and cook one minute, or until cheese melts.
6. Place on bun and enjoy with light condiments of your choice.

week 5

d a y 6

MAKE IT REAL: An Attitude of Gratitude

One important key to physical and emotional health (not to mention Christian health) is an attitude of gratitude. As the psalmist says, we are to come into God's presence giving Him thanks: "Enter his gates with thanksgiving and his courts with praise; give thanks to him and praise his name" (Psalm 100:4).

Obviously I don't know your physical, financial, or emotional status. You may be riding a great high in your life, or you might be in the deepest, darkest valley you've ever known. But as the gospel song says, "The God on the mountain is still God in the valley." Even in the times of greatest darkness, we have to cling to all the blessings we still have.

Gratitude promotes emotional growth and maturity. And there's another benefit—having an attitude of gratitude improves all your relationships too! Every relationship problem includes some aspect of failing to appreciate the other party. So learn to see with others' eyes, feel with their heart, and be thankful for what they add to your life.

A GRATITUDE ATTITUDE PAGE

Create a Gratitude Attitude page in your journal. Write down fifteen things you are grateful for.

Then, on the days when you feel that life is tearing you down or that you aren't making much progress, open your journal and read over those fifteen things. Add to the list during those times.

Most of all, be grateful for a Father who loves *you* and wants you to succeed!

week 5

d a y 7

A VOICE ALONG THE PATH: Kale's Story

Menu planning, ugh!

Who really has time to plan menus? I mean, does anyone, except maybe Martha Stewart, really plan an entire week's worth of meals? That is another one of those things that most diets require, and it's one of those things that never gets done. I guess that's why Weight Watchers and other diet plans that have pre-planned meals are so popular. But the trouble comes when they aren't around to plan your meals anymore.

I guess I don't like meal planning for a couple of reasons. First, it puts the person losing weight (me) in conflict with those not necessarily trying to lose weight (my family). When I roll out the salads and sugar-free Jell-O, they roll their eyes and remind me that they don't need to lose weight, thank you, so why should they suffer?

So I end up fixing two meals, one for me and one for them. Then, after a while, it's an entrée for me, and I'm eating their side dishes. And after a while, I'm eating the same old foods again, and gaining the same old weight.

Dr. Jantz suggested I involve the family this time, because it's not just about my weight loss. It's about establishing eating habits that mean healthier, longer lives for everyone in the family. Sure, they would rather keep eating the foods they're accustomed to, but we're trying to make a game out of finding new tastes that we like. If there is something we really love (like cheeseburgers), we find ways to reduce fat and keep the flavor. Our youngest, Wesley, came up with a brilliantly simple idea for that one—make the patties smaller! We used to form the patties by hand, so we got a hamburger press and made thinner patties, using about 1/8 of a pound of ground turkey rather than 1/4 pound of hamburger. The taste is the same, and the fat is greatly reduced.

Another area was mayonnaise. There was a general revolt about going to light mayonnaise, so we just use a lot less of the real thing on sandwiches, etc. When cooking, I'll cut the mayo in half and use fat-free sour cream as a substitute.

Our solutions aren't always perfect, but we are working at it. We even created a bonus for our kids' allowance if they can find one healthy recipe a week that we all like. Perhaps the biggest thing is that I have hope that my children won't ever have to go through the pain of being overweight if they learn about proper nutrition now. That's a gift that goes way beyond an extra dollar or two a week in allowance.

the total temple makeover

Therefore, since we are surrounded by such a great cloud of witnesses, let us throw off everything that hinders and the sin that so easily entangles, and let us run with perseverance the race marked out for us.

—Hebrews 12:1

STAYING THE COURSE
week 6
d a y 1

INSPIRATION: Patience

Consider these words from James 1:3–6:

> You know that the testing of your faith develops perseverance. Perseverance must finish its work so that you may be mature and complete, not lacking anything. If any of you lacks wisdom, he should ask God, who gives generously to all without finding fault, and it will be given to him. But when he asks, he must believe and not doubt, because he who doubts is like a wave of the sea, blown and tossed by the wind.

James reminds us that we need to live at God's pace, not ours. In today's world *patience* means waiting for someone to finish a sentence before we jump in to speak our point. We are incapable of even conceiving the patience of God, whose vision spans all eternity.

Think of all the times you have asked God for something. How long did you wait before you decided God didn't answer your prayer? A year? A month? An hour?

Sometimes I'm afraid we (and I include myself in this too) treat God as though heaven has a drive-thru window and the miracle we seek should be waiting at the window when we pull around.

Maybe the greatest miracle any of us can hope for is an understanding and acceptance of the will of God, Creator of the universe.

Then, perhaps, we can commit ourselves to living on *His* schedule, not our own.

I don't know where you are in your program as you read these words—perhaps things are going well for you . . . or perhaps not. Perhaps you have already given up and want to call it quits, but just feel compelled to finish the book. Whatever your situation, make the commitment to letting this program work for you at God's pace. Those God-ordained baby steps I keep talking about equal long-term success. So fix your eyes on the destination . . . and the One who awaits you at the finish line. Then run the race with patience.

week 6
d a y 2

DEVOTIONAL: Simply Trust
WHAT'S ON YOUR FRIDGE?

> Though I walk in the midst of trouble, you pre-
> serve my life . . . with your right hand you save
> me. The LORD will fulfill his purpose for me.
> (Psalm 138:7–8)

All of us are guilty of trying to make our faith conform to our
wants and desires. We talk about letting go and turning it over to
God, but we keep coming back in and grabbing the wheel away
from Him.

But God does things in His way and in His time. This week let
your prayers focus strongly on something many of us find very, very
hard to do: simply trusting God—placing ourselves fully and completely in His hands.

Dear Lord,

*It's so easy for me to want Your schedule to match up with
mine. I try to impose my will and my desires upon this life You
have given me. Give me strength, patience, and endurance to
run the race You have set before me. If I stumble or fall, please*

pick me up and put me right back on the path, continuing in the right direction.

You know how difficult it can be at times, Lord. Support me, lift me up, and fill me with Your Spirit so I will reach the goals I have set for better health, and so I may be a better servant and messenger of Your Word. Father, I am so grateful You are in my life. Amen.

week 6
d a y 3

THOUGHTS FOR FOOD: Getting Past the Plateau

Somewhere along the way, probably about now, you are going to reach "the dreaded plateau"—a point at which your weight feels "stuck."

That's one reason *The Total Temple Makeover* doesn't change you to a new diet all at once. Instead, I introduce changes into your diet gradually—for two reasons: (1) to allow your body to adjust to the dietary changes, and (2) to avoid the body settling into a new "set point."

Our bodies are marvels of self-regulation. As the amount of food we consume changes, our bodies change activity levels to match. A perfect example is the "starvation reflex." Overweight people often decide to make a drastic cut in the amount of calories they consume, sometimes cutting them by 50 percent or more. While this may result in a few days of rapid weight loss, pretty soon the starvation reflex kicks in. As your food intake falls, your body begins to use the remaining food more efficiently—thus burning fewer calories. This was intended to help our ancestors get through periods of famine, etc. If the starvation continues, the body will begin to use itself to power the body. Unfortunately, the body doesn't break down fat to power the body; the body breaks down the proteins—in other words, the muscle. Your body takes energy that has been stored as glycogen in the muscles and liver, then from fat in the fat cells. So if you are on a low-protein diet, your body actually feeds off your muscle tissue.

Of course, when we see our weight loss taper off, we tend to throw up our hands and go back to our old patterns of eating. But because our bodies are still in starvation mode for a time, we often put back on more weight than we have lost.

If you have hit a plateau, here is a simple little idea to help you break through.

Change Your Habits!

New Habit #6: Spend two to three days on the "S" plan.

The "S" plan is very simple: *Limit your diet to salads, soups, and cereals.* Don't load up on high-fat dressings or tons of cheese on your salads. Don't eat a lot of creamy soups—stick to the broth-based varieties. Don't eat the high-sugar cereals; favor the whole-grain ones already recommended. You should also increase your activity during this period.

After two to three days, no matter what your weight says, go back to your original eating plan. It might take a couple of attempts to break the plateau, but this should help reset your body's "thermostat" and get you back on the road to a healthy weight.

week 6
d a y 4

WHAT YOU EAT: Proteins

This week we explore another part of the four food groups—the proteins. The protein group includes all foods that are primary sources of protein: meats, nuts, dried beans, fish, and eggs. Proteins are commonly associated only with red and white meats, but nuts, soy, and beans are equally good sources of protein. The body uses protein in many different ways: to build new muscles or other tissues, to heal wounds and replace old tissues, to help fight infection, and to transport nutrients and oxygen in the blood. Amino acids are the building blocks of proteins. When amino acids are linked together in a chain, they form proteins. All but eight amino acids can be made by the body. These eight are called *essential amino acids* because they must be obtained from what you eat.

RED MEAT/PORK

We've all heard the horror stories about red meat and pork—sad to say, they are pretty accurate. A high consumption of red meat has been linked to heart problems, such as heart disease. Other diseases, such as E. coli, etc., can be attributed to the improper storage and preparation of red meats. However, other studies suggest that moderate consumption (one to two meals a week) of very lean red meat or pork, properly prepared and cooked, does not adversely affect weight loss or health.

FISH

One meat almost universally promoted is fish. Fish contains high levels of Omega-3 fats, and as you'll see in week 8, day 4, on oils and fats, this is one of the good fats that can help reduce the risk of heart disease. Fresh fish and seafood should make up a good portion of your meat diet.

For example, Eskimos in Greenland were found to have one-tenth of the heart attacks of the average U.S. population. Although their diet contained a great deal of fat, it came from cold water fish and seals. It was also found that they had low levels of LDL (bad) cholesterol and high levels of HDL (good) cholesterol. There is little doubt that their fish-rich diet (high in Omega-3 fatty acids) contributed to this phenomenon.

You should plan to include fish at least two to three times a week in your diet.

POULTRY

After fish, fresh poultry offers some of the best meat choices. Unfortunately, most of the poultry available is grown and processed by large conglomerates. The poultry are fed steroids, antibiotics, etc. They are also normally kept in confined spaces and given minimal exercise—this can result in a higher fat content. However, poultry still ranks better than beef in fat content and is a good option to substitute for beef. If available, choose kosher or free-range chicken, which tends to have fewer additives and lower fat.

EGGS

Many of the same cautions concerning poultry concern eggs as well. Eggs from organic farms and free-range chickens tend to carry less pesticides, antibiotics, and hormones than mass-produced varieties. Moderate consumption of eggs (no more than three to four per week) does not appear to adversely affect cholesterol levels as was once feared. Eggs are high in choline, an important fuel for brain function and memory. Some recent studies, while inconclusive, indicate that moderate consumption of eggs might even help reduce the risk of heart disease, due to the presence of lecithin.

DRIED BEANS AND NUTS

Soybeans are one of the wonder foods God placed on the earth. Soybeans contain protein that is similar in composition to meat protein.

Soy is a staple of the Japanese diet and is used in miso soup, tofu, soy milk, and other products. They consume about *forty times* the soy products we do in the U.S. It is likely no coincidence that Japanese have one-fourth the cases of breast and prostate cancer, since soy contains isoflavones, which can reduce the effect of estrogen on the body. Soy has also been linked to reduced side effects of menopause, calcium loss from osteoporosis, and numerous other benefits. Tofu is an extremely versatile form of soy that can be used to replace meat in many dishes.

Soy is one product that should definitely be added or increased in your diet, especially if you don't consume much now.

Other beans and nuts can be excellent sources of protein, but be aware of the high levels of fats some contain—especially nuts. However, peanuts and cashews have a low GL rating of 1–2. This is because most of the fats they contain are monounsaturated fats, the good fats. Yet even the good fats should be consumed in moderation. However, an occasional snack of nuts is fine.

AWE: Meats and Proteins		
avoid	**watch**	**eat**
Fatty red meat and pork	Lean red meat	Fish (especially those high in Omega-3 fats)
Processed meats, like bacon and sausage	Nuts	Dried beans
	Black-eyed peas	
Meats cooked with the skin	Lima beans	Soy protein
		Lentils
	Eggs	Free-range poultry

Figure 15.

week 6
d a y 5

THE JOURNEY JOURNAL: You're Halfway There

You are at the halfway point in your journey, so it's a good time to see just how far you've traveled.

Go back and look at the first week's journal entries and then complete the following worksheet.

WORKSHEET: The Halfway Check

Good changes I have seen since week 1

_____
_____
_____
_____

Bad changes since week 1

_____
_____
_____
_____

Ways I can further improve what I have done so far

_____
_____
_____
_____
_____
_____
_____

The changes I'll make this week to get better

_____
_____
_____
_____
_____

I am committed to going the distance, and I reaffirm that by signing and dating the following statement in my journal.

"With God I am going the distance."

Signature: _____

Date: _____

Don't forget to spend time in your personal journal!

week 6
d a y 6

MAKE IT REAL: Simple Food Revisions Can Make a Difference

What are two or three of your favorite or most common meals? (If there are several members of your household, ask each person what his or her favorite meals are.)

There are all sorts of ways to make small changes in these meals in order to bring them more into alignment with your new eating guidelines.

To get you started, see the sample Food Revision Chart below. I've shown what you can do with a very common meal—hamburgers!

Food Revision Chart: Hamburger & French Fries

Original Ingredients	Fit and Faithful Ingredients
1/4 lb. ground beef patty, pan fried	Mix of 1/8 lb. lean ground beef and 1/8 lb. ground turkey, grilled or baked
Hamburger bun	Whole-grain bun
Cheese	Thin slice of hard cheese
Mayo	Light mayo

Figure 16.

Ready to try it yourself? There is a blank form in appendix F for you to copy and use. Write the ingredients of each meal in the boxes under Original Ingredients. In the boxes under Fit and Faithful Ingredients, write down some changes you can make to the dish or meal to make it more in line with your new eating guidelines. Don't worry if it doesn't create the "perfect" food. Simply look for ways to make it better than how you eat it today.

week 6

d a y 7

A VOICE ALONG THE PATH: Kale's Story

Halfway there.

This is still unlike any diet I've ever been on. I know, I know. It's not a diet. Dr. Jantz keeps telling me that. I guess we'll call it what he calls it—a life plan. I feel like I should be following this menu, doing that exercise, etc. I feel like there are too many choices left up to me. Dr. J says that's the point. That for too long, over-weight people have wanted someone else to take control, to tell them what to eat, how to exercise, and so on. The problem is that when the traditional diet is over and people have to take control of their own lives, they feel lost.

I like the analogy he used. Of course. It was a food analogy.

"Suppose you came to me and said, 'I want to learn to cook like a great chef.' I take you into the kitchen and teach you how to make a wonderful soup. I then teach you to make a delicious appe-tizer, then a stunning main course, finally a scrumptious dessert. You have your friends over for dinner one evening and cook all those dishes, and they are positively floored. They can't wait to be invited back. You come back to me and tell of your success. I shake your hand and tell you congratulations, and send you on your way.

"But what will you fix at the next dinner? I taught you how to cook a great meal, but I haven't taught you to be a great chef.

"Traditional diets do the same thing. They teach you how to eat during the diet, but they don't teach you how to make intelligent, healthy choices. They don't teach you how to deal with the emotional, as well as the physical, changes you need to go through. And they certainly don't teach you how to reconcile all this within your Christian life."

I guess he was saying that I have to make my own decisions, chart my own way. He can give me tools and information to make sound, spiritual decisions, but the responsibility for making those decisions lies with me.

And the only one who should be in control of my life, other than me, is God.

the total temple makeover

In him the whole building is joined together and rises to become a holy temple in the Lord.

—Ephesians 2:21

FOOD, FITNESS, AND THE FATHER

week 7

day 1

INSPIRATION: Fulfilling Your Purpose

The Web site dictionary.com defines *fitness* as follows:

> **fit·ness** *n.* **1.** The state or condition of being fit; suitability or appropriateness. **2.** Good health or physical condition, especially as the result of exercise and proper nutrition.

In the previous weeks, I've talked about fitness as described in the second definition above. This week, however, let's consider the first definition.

HOW AND WHERE DO YOU FIT?

All of us spend a lot of time thinking about if we *are* fit, but as Christians we don't spend nearly enough time asking ourselves *how* and *where* we fit, in relation to God's plan.

Paul beautifully expressed this idea of finding your place in God's plan in 1 Corinthians 12. This concept is so important, let's read the entire chapter.

> Now about spiritual gifts, brothers, I do not want you to be ignorant. You know that when you were pagans, somehow or other you were influenced and led astray to mute idols. Therefore I tell you that no one who is speaking by the Spirit

of God says, "Jesus be cursed," and no one can say, "Jesus is Lord," except by the Holy Spirit.

There are different kinds of gifts, but the same Spirit. There are different kinds of service, but the same Lord. There are different kinds of working, but the same God works all of them in all men.

Now to each one the manifestation of the Spirit is given for the common good. To one there is given through the Spirit the message of wisdom, to another the message of knowledge by means of the same Spirit, to another faith by the same Spirit, to another gifts of healing by that one Spirit, to another miraculous powers, to another prophecy, to another distinguishing between spirits, to still another the interpretation of tongues. All these are the work of one and the same Spirit, and he gives them to each one, just as he determines.

The body is a unit, though it is made up of many parts; and though all its parts are many, they form one body. So it is with Christ. For we were all baptized by one Spirit into one body— whether Jews or Greeks, slave or free—and we were all given the one Spirit to drink.

Now the body is not made up of one part but of many. If the foot should say, "Because I am not a hand, I do not belong to the body," it would not for that reason cease to be part of the body. And if the ear should say, "Because I am not an eye, I do not belong to the body," it would not for that reason cease to be part of the body. If the whole body were an eye, where would the sense of hearing be? If the whole body were an ear, where would the sense of smell be? But in fact God has arranged the parts in the body, every one of them, just as he wanted them to be. If they were all one part, where would the body be? As it is, there are many parts, but one body.

The eye cannot say to the hand, "I don't need you!" And the head cannot say to the feet, "I don't need you!" On the contrary, those parts of the body that seem to be weaker are indispensable, and the parts that we think are less honorable we treat with special honor. And the parts that are unpresentable are treated with special modesty, while our presentable parts need no special treatment. But God has combined the members of the body and has given greater honor to the parts that lacked it, so that there should be no division in the body, but that its parts should have equal concern for each other. If one part suffers, every part suffers with it; if one part is honored, every part rejoices with it.

Now you are the body of Christ, and each one of you is a part of it. And in the church God has appointed first of all apostles, second prophets, third teachers, then workers of miracles, also those having gifts of healing, those able to help others, those with gifts of administration, and those speaking in different kinds of tongues. Are all apostles? Are all prophets? Are all teachers? Do all work miracles? Do all have gifts of healing? Do all speak in tongues? Do all interpret? But eagerly desire the greater gifts.

God has a reason for creating you. There is a purpose you are supposed to fulfill. What is it? How do you go about finding it?

Paul gives us the answers within this text.

What gifts has God given you? What are you passionate about in life (or what did you used to be passionate about)?

God didn't place that gift and that passion in you for nothing.

Spend some time today thinking about why God gave you the skills He did and how you can use them to further His kingdom.

week 7
d a y 2

DEVOTIONAL: God's Plan for You

WHAT'S ON YOUR FRIDGE?

> He who began a good work in you will carry it on
> to completion until the day of Christ Jesus.
> (Philippians 1:6)

Just as you need a strong sense of purpose to meet your health goals, you need a strong sense of purpose to meet God's goals in *all* phases of your life.

Each of us fits into God's plan, and it is part of our purpose to find out where and how. As you reshape your own body this week, remember to also reshape your role as a part of the body of Christ.

Dear God,

Thank You for the passion, which fills my heart. Thank You for the longing for You, which fills my soul. Thank You for the desire to do Your will, which guides my steps. Each day, make me a better instrument of Your work. As You see fit: Temper me with difficulties, strengthen me with adversity, comfort me with love, direct me with compassion, teach me with understanding. I exist to further Your kingdom. Help me to better do Your work each day to the end of my days, till You walk upon this earth again. Amen.

week 7
d a y 3

THOUGHTS FOR FOOD: Dairy-Based Treats

Ever get an urge for a really good dessert or snack? Like one of those frothy milk shakes? Mmm . . .

WHAT? NO MILK SHAKES?

Although I'll address desserts and snacks more fully in a later chapter, I'll touch briefly on dairy-based treats and similar snack items in this chapter. But don't despair. I'm not heartless.

We all get the urge for a little something sweet from time to time, and you shouldn't deny yourself an occasional little treat. It is when you force yourself to abstain completely that you eventually reach a point of frustration with typical diets and go off them. For most people, going off means returning completely to bad eating habits. But you don't have to fall into that trap.

CHANGE YOUR HABITS!

New Habit #7: Remember that one slip doesn't make you a failure.

There is nothing wrong with taking a "vacation" from a proper diet once in a while. In other words, if you've been good for seven weeks and would really like to have a chocolate peanut-butter milk shake, then for heaven's sake, have one. Naturally, you should try to use nonfat yogurt, if available, and make the best choices available for ingredients, but after that just have the treat and be done with it. No burden of guilt, no great anxiety. Just admit you had a moment of indulgence and move on with your program.

Our goal together is to remove any emotional "land mines" that may have caused you in the past to fail to make meaningful change, and strict denial is one that many have found to simply be too hard to adhere to.

It's OK to have a bad snack in a weak moment. What *isn't* acceptable is allowing one slip to make you believe you're a full-blown failure.

If you have kids, go on a "treasure hunt" with them to find healthy snack alternatives to help them begin to see there are options that can be healthier and good tasting.

Here's one to get you started.

Fruit Smoothie

Ingredients
1 cup of skim milk
3 ice cubes
Your favorite fresh fruit

Instructions
1. Blend in a blender.
2. Add a dash of vanilla, cinnamon, and nutmeg.[2]

For even better smoothies, consider a supplement like UltraMeal. It's a special body-composition formula designed for fast assimilation and to improve metabolism. Visit www.aplaceofhope.com for more information.

week 7

d a y   4

WHAT YOU EAT: Dairy

A common source of protein for Americans is dairy products. However, the proverbial wisdom about the benefits of drinking milk each day is now being questioned, especially for adults.

Milk can be a good source of calcium and nutrients for growing young people, but can have adverse effects on adults. Walter Willett, chair of the Department of Nutrition at Harvard School of Public Health, stated in an article in the November 2002 edition of *Harvard Public Health* that consumption of two to three glasses of milk a day could promote increased incidence of prostate cancer in men and breast cancer in women.

Even with the increased availability of nonfat and low-fat milk, 12 percent of the typical American's fat consumption comes from dairy products. In addition, more and more Americans are finding out they have sensitivities to dairy products and/or are lactose intolerant.

If you suspect allergies might be contributing to your weight and health problems, an excellent resource is *The Food Allergy Cure: A New Solution to Food Cravings, Obesity, Depression, Headaches, Arthritis, and Fatigue.*[1]

A large source of dairy fat is cheese. Even though most dairy products have a low GL rating (usually under 10) and can be a good source of protein, certain B vitamins, and calcium, the concerns about milk mentioned already and their general high level of fats make dairy products a group you should consume in moderation. The one exception is low-fat yogurt, especially plain yogurt without added sweeteners (add your own fresh fruit). In addition to calcium, it is rich in vitamins A and B and in lactic acid. Plain yogurt with herbs and spices added makes an excellent salad dressing.

AWE: Dairy Products		
avoid	watch	eat
Whole milk	Low-fat milk	Plain yogurt
Soft cheese	Hard cheeses	Skim (nonfat) milk
Processed cheese foods	Ice milk (nonfat)	
Ice cream		

Figure 17.

week 7
d a y 5

THE JOURNEY JOURNAL: Your Reason for Being

Purpose. It seems to be something we should all give a lot of thought to—our purpose for being. It's something God has given a lot of thought to: "In him we were also chosen, having been predestined according to the plan of him who works out everything in conformity with the purpose of his will" (Ephesians 1:11).

Yet how many simply exist, as though existence itself were enough of a purpose?

Deciding and defining the reason for your being is not like a homework assignment—get the right answer and you are done. Just like creating a new health style, defining your purpose requires you to change the way you think about life. It also requires you to frequently ask God about His purpose for you. Has that purpose changed? Do you need to modify your life to better meet His needs?

Spend some time in your journal considering God's purpose for you. I'd also recommend you read *The Purpose-Driven Life* by Rick Warren, for additional help in divining God's role for you to play in this majestic tapestry called life.

WORKSHEET: Discovering My Purpose

As you answer the following questions, take the time to give them the thought they deserve, then sleep on the answers. The next day read them again, then revisit them often, and modify them as needed.

What skills and gifts has God blessed me with? _____

_____

_____

_____

_____

_____

What activities and subjects do I feel passion or intense curiosity about?

_____

_____

_____

_____

_____

_____

_____

*In what ways could I combine my skills and passions?*_____

_____

_____

_____

_____

_____

*How could I use those combinations for God's glory and to further His kingdom?*_____

_____

_____

_____

_____

_____

week 7
d a y 6

MAKE IT REAL: Try Something New!

Ready for both a mental and physical challenge? Then here it is: find and try three new forms of exercise or activities this week. These should be exercises or activities that you can do alone or with others and should provide you with a new experience. Here are some suggestions to get you started thinking:

- ◆ Tai Chi—(a moving form of meditation)
- ◆ Wall Climbing—(a challenging simulation of mountain climbing, found at some health clubs)
- ◆ Dancing—(ballet, belly, swing, salsa, square, ballroom, country line, etc.) Grab that dancing partner, and sign up for a free lesson!
- ◆ Martial Arts and Self-Defense—(an exercise of self-protection based on techniques developed in ancient China, India, and Tibet)
- ◆ Medicine Ball—(a weighted ball used in physical training)
- ◆ Pilates (a method of flexibility and strength training that focuses on strengthening the abdominal core)
- ◆ Synchronized Swimming—(a water sport with coordinated dancelike movements set to music)
- ◆ TaeBo (aerobics and self-defense)

You can get videos from the library, attend a local club or school, or ask friends who might participate in the activity. Other good sources are Web sites, such as www.victoriajohnson.com or www.taebo.com.

So shake off the dust, and shake up your activity routine. You just might find a new form of activity that you can enjoy the rest of your life!

week 7
d a y 7

A VOICE ALONG THE PATH: Kale's Story

Well, I tried something new this week—Tai Chi. The only thing I really knew about it was from what I've seen on TV commercials and so on. It turns out it is very involved; it's almost more like a dance than exercise.

Anyway, I had pulled a calf muscle last week moving some furniture around, so I needed to avoid anything real strenuous, and Dr. Jantz recommended I try this. It doesn't really feel like exercise, since you don't work up a sweat. At the end, though, I have to admit I felt a lot calmer and less stressed. I can also see how bad my flexibility had become from being a couch potato. Tai Chi will definitely help with that. With having to think so much about getting the proper form and balance, there's no time for the normal day's thoughts to break in. I enjoyed it, and I think I'll add it to my exercise "toolbox." It's a nice change from strenuous activities.

The other part of my "growing" this week was a lot tougher—working on my purpose. Between you and me, Journal, I'm not sure God really has a purpose for me. I don't have any outstanding skills. I love music, but I'm not a great musician or singer. I enjoy painting, but I'm no Thomas Kinkade. I like being with kids and helping out some of the older members of the church, but I don't have some shining skill that I can use for God's glory.

Dr. J said that the purpose is not to do grand works in God's name, but to do great works. He pointed out that Jesus didn't heal Caesar or Pontius Pilate; he healed the average person in the street. He didn't raise Caesar from the dead, but his friend Lazarus and an unknown little girl. He didn't feed the Senate of Rome with a miracle, but a throng of common folk on a dusty hillside. Jesus used his gifts on "plain" people, because great works aren't great because of who notices them.

The universe is God's tapestry, and we are the threads He weaves in His great design. No thread—whether it is the brightest red or the dullest gray—contributes to the tapestry more than another. The key is to find your place, your "fit," in the tapestry.

I'm still not sure where my place is just yet. But I'm thinking. I'm searching. And when the time is right, God will reveal it to me, I'm sure.

Search me, O God, and know my heart: test me, and know my anxious thoughts.

—Psalm 139:23

LIVING WITH YOURSELF
week 8
d a y 1

INSPIRATION: Overcoming Mind Enemies

No one would pretend that changing something as basic as the way you consume and burn off calories is going to be easy. There will be many obstacles in your path.

Well-meaning people will try to get you to do the wrong things. Enemies will try to stop you.

Your biggest enemy is yourself.

You are fighting against every failed attempt that has come before. You are fighting against every moment of low self-esteem, every pang of guilt, every negative thought that led you to be overweight in the first place.

If you are still struggling at this point, it may be time to take the kid gloves off and deal strongly with those "mind enemies" that have alienated you from yourself and from the person you wish to be.

If you need to, go back and read over the Inspiration in chapter 4, day 1. Do any of those mental "traps" still have a hold on you? If so, make them a focus of your prayers and thoughts this week.

If you are struggling particularly with certain thoughts and emotions that are holding you back, take the time to discuss them with your minister or pastor. As your spiritual advisor, he or she can help you put your struggles in a Christian context.

God never said we wouldn't have struggles. Indeed, trials and struggles are one way in which God molds us into what He would have us be. Remember, being healthy and losing weight will be one of your greatest personal accomplishments. You will reclaim your own life!

week 8
d a y 2

DEVOTIONAL: The Gift of Faith

WHAT'S ON YOUR FRIDGE?

> These have come so that your faith—of greater
> worth than gold, which perishes even though
> refined by fire—may be proved genuine and may
> result in praise, glory and honor when Jesus Christ
> is revealed. (1 Peter 1:7)

Do you ever wonder why God allows His children to go through
trials and hard times? Deep down you already know the answer. Just
as steel tempered in the fire is made stronger, coming through your
own "fires" makes you a stronger and better tool to be wielded by
God's hand.

In short, if faith were easy, it wouldn't be faith!

This week, let's pray for some gifts that really matter—faith and
belief.

Dear God,

You know what is in my heart and in my mind. I desire to
improve my body, so I may run the race You set before me. I desire
to improve my health, that I might give testament to Your goodness.
I desire a full life, that I might lead others to Your glory. In You are

all things created and are all things possible. When You need to try me, fill me also with faith. When the darkness of doubt surrounds me, lift me into the light of belief. When I threaten to stumble on the path You would have me walk, steady me with Your loving hand. And in all these things, let me know Your purpose and plan for me as You will, so I may be what You would have me be, do what You would have me do, and go where You would have me go. Amen.

week 8
d a y 3

THOUGHTS FOR FOOD: Eating Alone

What's your greatest danger zone?

Eating alone! It's too easy to plunk down in front of the TV with a sandwich and a bag of potato chips. A half hour later, the sandwich, the chips, and your self-esteem have all been consumed.

It's simply too easy to not think about what you are eating when you eat alone. So make a special effort to put systems in place to keep you from falling into the "home alone" trap.

Of course, if you live alone, you have a lot of opportunities to eat badly, so the tips and techniques below apply even more to you.

CHANGE YOUR HABITS!

New Habit #8: Make meals for one healthy.

Here are some ideas for making meals for one healthy:

- If you don't bring it home, you can't eat it. The place to stop the impulse eating of snack cakes and other nutrient-poor foods is at the grocery store, not as you are heading for the cupboard.
- Buy healthy foods and break them down into single servings. For example, buy a tuna steak, divide it into two-ounce servings in sandwich bags, and put the bags in the freezer.

That makes it easy to add fish to a meal for one. You can do the same thing with vegetable medleys, etc.

- Soups, stews, and Crockpot dishes make excellent multiday meals.
- Fresh beans, lentils, and green vegetables can easily be separated into single servings.
- There is nothing wrong with having a sandwich, as long as you stick to the "E" foods from the AWE lists and avoid the mayo, etc.
- Single meals are a great time to practice food-combination techniques and to implement eating several small meals instead of one large one. Avoid the temptation to turn two servings of food into one big stomachache.
- Don't eat in front of the TV.
- Eat outside, if possible.
- Combine the meal with a leisurely walk. Get the best of both worlds!

Meals for one can be healthy, delicious, and keep you moving toward your goal.

If you find some particular recipes that you enjoy, share them with us at mystory@aplaceofhope.com.

week 8

d a y 4

WHAT YOU EAT: Fats and Oils

The final part of the food pyramid is the one that nutritionists stress should make up the smallest part of your diet—fats and oils.

The general consensus for a long time was that fats and oils are all bad and lead to weight problems, as well as being damaging to the heart and other organs of the body.

Today, however, we know that the picture simply isn't that black and white. To be sure, many fats should not even be considered in a healthy diet. But science is now finding that other fats and oils may actually promote good health.

WHAT TO AVOID

Let's start with the fats and oils you should avoid.

Most cooking oils and those used in mass-produced foods are seed oils. Oils processed in large factories are obtained by crushing the oil-bearing seeds and heating them to about 230 degrees Fahrenheit. The oil is then squeezed out at extremely high pressure, which generates more heat.

In order to extract the last 10 percent or so of the oil from crushed seeds, processors treat the pulp with one of a number of solvents—usually hexane (which is similar to gasoline). The solvent is then boiled off, although up to 100 parts per million may remain in the oil. Such solvents, themselves toxic, also retain the toxic pesticides that were in the seeds and grains before processing begins.

High-temperature processing causes the weak carbon bonds of some fatty acids to break apart, thereby creating dangerous free radicals. In addition, antioxidants, such as fat-soluble vitamin E, which protects the body from free radicals, are neutralized or destroyed by high temperatures and pressures. BHT and BHA (artificial preservatives) are often added to these oils to replace vitamin E and other natural preservatives destroyed by heat.

What Is Preferred

However, there is an alternative to the common method of processing oils. These are oils that are produced using an expeller method. Expeller processed oils are not subjected to heat and solvents but to a strictly mechanical pressure to remove the oil. These oils (called virgin or "cold-pressed" oils) should be preferred.

Beware of Hydrogenation

Oils are turned into solid and semisolid fats (like margarine and shortening) by a process called *hydrogenation*, which we have briefly discussed before in week 3, day 4. To produce them, manufacturers begin with the most inexpensive oils—soy, corn, cottonseed, or canola, already rancid from the extraction process—and mix them with tiny metal particles, usually nickel oxide. The oil with its nickel catalyst is then subjected to hydrogen gas in a high-pressure, high-temperature reactor.

Next, emulsifiers and starch are squeezed into the mixture to give it a better consistency. To remove the unpleasant odor, the oil is steam-cleaned at high temperatures. Margarine's natural gray color is removed by bleach, and then dyes and flavors are added to make it resemble butter. Finally, the mixture is compressed and packaged in blocks or tubs. (For more on hydrogenation, see www.americanheart.org and enter "hydrogenation" in the search text box.)

Trans-fats are the result of partial hydrogenation. Literally, trans-fats are toxins the body treats as organic fats and introduces into the body, along with the toxins they carry. Trans-fats are especially dangerous because they raise the LDL (bad) cholesterol while lowering the HDL (good) cholesterol. When reading a food label, you might notice that the total fat listed in the food is higher than the sum of all the fats listed. The bulk of that difference is trans-fats. Until trans-fats are listed on the food label (which will be in 2006), you should use this method to calculate the amount of trans-fats in the foods you eat.

There is almost universal agreement in the health community that any movement to healthier eating habits should include reducing trans-fatty acids in your diet.

In general, avoid oils that contain high levels of saturated fats. On the other hand, unsaturated fats have been found to have positive health benefits, such as lowering cholesterol levels, and should make up the bulk of the oils you do consume.

One final oil that should be mentioned is fish oil, which contains the Omega-3 fatty acids. These acids provide a wealth of health benefits. Interestingly, it turns out that the old adage about fish being brain food has some basis in fact, as Omega-3 acids have been shown to improve brain function. They also lower cholesterol and triglycerides, improve blood sugar, and reduce artery and heart disease and lower blood pressure. If fish (or at least fish-oil supplements) are not a part of your regular diet, it's time to incorporate them. Canola and soybean oil are also good sources for Omega-3 acids. The only caveat against increasing your consumption of Omega-3 acids is if you have problems with "thin" blood, as Omega-3 will reduce clotting capability.

For cooking, you can't choose better oil than extra virgin olive oil. The people of Jesus's time highly prized the use of olive oil, and with good reason. It is one of the healthiest vegetable oils available. It has been shown to improve cholesterol levels, stimulate digestion, and reduce the risk of heart disease. Olive oil and olive-oil-based products like Olivio should be your number one choice for cooking. Use them as a substitute for butter and other shortenings.

AWE: Fats and Oils		
avoid	**watch**	**eat**
Coconut oil	Corn oil	Olive oil
Palm kernel	Peanut oil	Canola oil
Hydrogenated oils	Safflower oil	Fish oil
Partially hydrogenated oils	Sesame oil	Soybean oil
Margarine	Sunflower oil	
Butter		

Figure 18.

week 8
d a y 5

THE JOURNEY JOURNAL: Just Try It!

Using the right types of oils and fats in your diet is one of the biggest keys to eating healthy, so here is your journal exercise for the week. Just Try It!

◆ Pick a favorite recipe (e.g., bread or a favorite dish) that you can make in single meal portions. Try the recipe with olive oil and at least one other of the recommended oils to see which ones you like better.

◆ Try using olive oil in several of your recipes this week. It is extremely important that you make the move away from butter and margarine to oils that are made up primarily of unsaturated fats.

◆ Come up with at least two fish dishes this week that make use of what are called high-fat fish. Don't be put off by the name, because the high fat is Omega-3. These include salmon, mackerel, and herring.

◆ Record your new recipes in your journal and look for other ways to continue your move towards putting more healthy fats in your diet.

week 8
d a y 6

MAKE IT REAL: Share Your Health

Up to now much of the focus has been on you, your thoughts, your feelings, and the changes you need to go through. And that's the way it should be, since change begins within before the first external changes are visible.

Hopefully you have seen the changes in yourself. You *think differently* about food, about exercise, about the purpose for your body and life. If so, I rejoice in these changes with you.

This week it's time to share these thoughts with that overweight friend you've been thinking about. Maybe it's your best friend, maybe it's someone at your church, or maybe it's your spouse. However, I can almost guarantee that as you're reading this, one friend in particular comes to mind. And you think, he/she needs this.

Start the process this week of introducing that friend to what you have learned. Perhaps he's noticed a change and has been asking you about it. You may even have discussed it with her already. Now is a good time to start helping that friend down the path you are walking.

How do you start? Simple—invite them over for dinner when you are serving one of your "new way" meals. Invite them out to play tennis, or some other activity you've discovered. If they aren't attending a church regularly, and your church has put together a weight loss group, then invite them to a meeting.

Encourage them to get the book and start reading it, and offer to help them along, as perhaps someone else is helping you along.

Part of being a child of God means learning to live in His family—and that includes helping others reach their goals and find their life purpose for Christ. Start that process this week, today, right now, and stay true to the path!

And do it now, before that person develops health issues (which they WILL) or even dies. For them, but also for yourself, have that talk you've always wanted to have.

With whom will you talk this week? Write that name in your journal.

week 8

d a y 7

A VOICE ALONG THE PATH: Kale's Story

I talked to my brother today.

You would have thought I was asking him about a drug addiction he might have or a criminal record. That was how nervous and embarrassed I felt.

We have always been a hefty family, but my brother was the undisputed champ. None of us knew exactly what he weighed (we would have been afraid to ask), but there was no doubt that it was well over three hundred pounds.

Anyway, he made a comment today about the weight I had lost and then mentioned how he wished he could lose a little weight.

At the time he and I were sitting alone on the front porch. I had watched him painfully struggle down to sit on the step, knowing how much pain his feet had been giving him lately.

"It's killing you, you know."

He looked up at me sharply. I had been quiet a long time before speaking, and I found that I could not meet his eyes, at least not yet. I took a deep breath, then plunged in before I could change my mind.

"Almost every health problem you have is either caused or made worse by the weight you carry around," I said. "And it's going to kill you sooner rather than later." Finally, I looked up and met his gaze.

Now it was his turn to look away. "I know," he replied sadly. "And I really wish I could do something about it. But I'm afraid it's already too late for me."

Oh, no. I had opened my big mouth now, and I wasn't going to let it go that easy. "You know, God doesn't want you to commit suicide, and that's what you are doing. Just as sure as a gun to your head or a needle in your arm—it's suicide."

He bristled, "Wait a minute—"

I interrupted. "You know I'm right! How many doctors have to tell you what it's doing to you for it to be clear? Maybe it's not even your fault, but it is your problem, and you're the only one who can decide if you are going to change it."

"God has a much bigger purpose for you in life, but you have to be here to find out what it is and to make it happen. I'll help you, and you can help me to continue. I don't know that we'll succeed, but I do know we can't if we aren't even willing to start, to make the effort."

He shook his head slowly, "I don't know."

I smiled. "Neither do I. But God does. Let's just make a start, and we'll leave the knowing part to Him."

the total temple makeover

Each helps the other and says to his brother, "Be strong!"

—Isaiah 41:6

LIVING WITH OTHERS
week 9
d a y 1

INSPIRATION: Social Interactions

Being a Christian means joining the family of God, becoming a part of His church family. For many, the church becomes the hub of their social lives. And a lot of that social activity involves food—picnics, celebrations, potluck dinners.

THE CHURCH AND FOOD CONNECTION

The church has a long history with meals. From the sharing of the first fruit (unfortunately, forbidden) to the Last Supper, food plays an integral role in the Bible. Therefore, it's natural that meals would also make up a large part of church life.

However, this is a case where "partaking fully" of church life might not be the best thing for your continued spiritual and physical improvement. Rather than succumb to the temptation of eating Mrs. Magillicutti's delicious fudge brownies, use these meals as a chance to introduce fellow church members to your own new healthy cooking. Whip up a delicious low-fat dish, and show the other members of your church how healthy eating doesn't mean giving up taste. Part of our responsibility of being a Christian is to help other Christians improve mentally, spiritually, and physically. Take this opportunity to share what you have learned with others and to make healthy food fun!

For scrumptious low-fat recipes, visit www.aplaceofhope.com. For a wonderful, low-fat cookbook, I heartily recommend *Graham Kerr's Best: A Low-Fat, Heart Healthy Cookbook*.[1]

While on the subject of sharing, remember that it's not only your fellow Christians who can benefit from your experience. As you lose weight and inches, you have no doubt started to get comments from others. When they ask what you are doing, tell them, and explain how working on your spirit, as well as your body, has made a difference in your whole life, not just in your eating habits. You don't have to preach at them or make a production out of witnessing to them, simply share the good news you have enjoyed over the course of these twelve weeks, and encourage them to read the book as well. Who knows what seeds your example can plant in others? "Set an example for the believers in speech, in life, in love, in faith, and in purity" (1 Timothy 4:12).

HANDLING INCREASED ATTENTION

There is, however, another aspect of your new image that you will have to guard against. As you lose weight, you may find yourself uncomfortable with the fact that more members of the opposite sex are noticing you. Somehow the idea of becoming more sexually appealing invokes images that don't fit well with a sincere Christian desire to improve your health. (If this is a real issue for you, check out my book *Too Close to the Flame*[2] from www.aplaceofhope.com.)

It is a fact that all persons who are successful in losing weight must face this increased attention at some point. How they handle it is an important factor in their ability to continue to see improvement. For some, the extra weight has been something of a shield, a way to avoid having to consider the idea of relationships, which they have never handled very well. Faced with this newfound popularity, some retreat to the "sanctuary" of being overweight and undo all the good work they have accomplished.

Others react in the opposite manner, letting the reactions play on their vanity. Sadly, they may find themselves falling into unhealthy relationships, even to the point of destroying their existing relationships. This verse from John gives us wonderful insight into how we should deal with this issue: "For everything in the world—the cravings of sinful man, the lust of his eyes and the boasting of what he has and does—comes not from the Father but from the world" (1 John 2:16).

It is not wrong to take pleasure in improving your body, for you are improving God's gift to you. However, you have to always be on guard that this very simple pleasure doesn't shift to pride and vanity. Always remind yourself how temporary and fleeting the entire world is. Its existence is but a blink of God's eye. Like all of humankind, you have a part to play on this stage we call life, but always remember just how short this play is in comparison to what follows.

So take compliments graciously. Don't minimize what you have done—but don't pat yourself on the back. Simply say, "Thank you," and in your heart praise God. Give thanks for the strength and support for what you have achieved and what you *will* achieve in His name.

week 9
d a y 2

DEVOTIONAL: Keeping Your Spiritual Focus
WHAT'S ON YOUR FRIDGE?

> Remove far from me vanity and lies: give me neither poverty nor riches; feed me with food convenient for me. (Proverbs 30:8 KJV)

How can you live in the world, while keeping your mind, your soul, and your body fixed on the work of the Father? It is a day-by-day and moment-by-moment choice to focus your eyes on the prize that awaits us at the end of our brief work on this earth.

Heavenly Father,

You are eternal. You are the Creator of the universe. Your hand held the stars, and a sweep of Your arm formed the universe. Forgive me when my mind dwells on the miniscule, the tiny aspects of my life. In those times when I question, reassure me. In those times when I falter, lift me up. In those times when I despair, comfort me. Help me to be accepting of the fact that I am not capable of knowing all Your plans for me. Make it sufficient for me to know Your will for me, and give me the strength and resolve to do as You will. In all my dealings with others, Christian and non-Christian alike, help me to be a witness and an example of one who strives to do Your work and follow Your path. Let them see You through me and my life, so that they may know Your grace. Help me to have a healthy appreciation for who You made me to be, to be proud of your creation, and to love my body as You wish me to. Amen.

week 9
d a y 3

THOUGHTS FOR FOOD: Supplements

What vitamin and mineral supplements should you take, and in what form? How do you know if you are even taking the right things for your body?

First and foremost, get an assessment of your present status by visiting your doctor. Doctors can do a nutritional profile to see where your body is. It is an ironic fact that many overweight people suffer some vitamin deficiencies, simply because they eat too much of the wrong things. Your doctor would be in the best position to tell you if you suffer from any severe vitamin deficiencies.

CHANGE YOUR HABITS!

New Habit #9: Include vitamin supplements in your diet.

Before going any further, I should make one thing clear: the BEST—and most preferred—source for vitamins, minerals, and other nutrients is a healthy, balanced diet. Eating the proper mix of the right foods should supply you with most of the nutrients your body requires.

However, all of us tend to fall short in the nutrient department in some way. Recently, the American Medical Association (AMA) determined that everyone would likely benefit from supplements to ensure a proper minimum balance of vitamins, minerals, and nutrients. It's no wonder the vitamin and supplement industry is huge, with sales totaling over $5.5 billion a year in the U.S. alone.

So, what kind of supplements should you consider? What nutritional supplements do most overweight people need?

- *An adequate intake of water.* This is so important that I'm repeating it here, even though water is not a vitamin or supplement. Water is the basic building block of organic life— it is the medium through which nutrients are carried throughout the body. A person who has an inadequate water intake cannot achieve full health. If you have been neglecting your water, get back on the program! This is especially important for older individuals. Older people tend to have a diminished sense of thirst, so they will not intake adequate amounts of water even if they are exerting themselves. It's important to do the DEW (as in **D**rink **E**nough **W**ater!). At least 32 oz. per day—more if you are attempting to lose weight.

- *Fiber.* It is very common for overweight people to get inadequate amounts of dietary fiber. Adding whole grains, high-fiber natural cereals, and fresh vegetables should go a long way to ensuring you get adequate fiber—especially insoluble fiber. However, if you find it necessary to supplement, choose a natural fiber product.

- *Vitamins C and D.* Usually overweight people are not big on fruits (no, banana splits don't count), so they may not be getting enough of these vitamins.

- *Omega-3 fatty acids.* You're wondering, "Did I read that right? He's saying I may not be getting enough of a type of fat?" That's right. Overweight people tend to be red-meat consumers; fish doesn't make up a large part of their diet. Therefore, they may not be getting enough of this essential fatty acid, which can help improve heart health. If you simply can't abide fish (or you don't trust your local supplies) then look for a good Omega-3 supplement. Warning: All fish oil tablets do NOT necessarily contain the proper amount of Omega-3, so check the labels.

- *Conjugated Linoleic Acid.* CLA is a natural fatty acid that is important for cell membrane structure and cell communications. Research conducted at the University of Wisconsin discovered that CLA can significantly reduce body fat while increasing muscle mass. It is also a potent antioxidant, protecting body cells from the damaging effects of free radicals (the byproduct of oxidation). CLA occurs naturally in red meat and dairy foods. Most CLA supplements are derived from natural plant oils.

See www.aplaceofhope.com for several supplements specifically for weight regulation and obesity. Check them out, especially the Ultra-Meal supplements. Also online is a nutritional test you can take (it's free, so why not take advantage of it?). After taking the test, you will obtain a report that can serve as a starting place to improve your nutritional balance.

Supplements can be a good support to a healthy diet, but your goal should be to eat in a manner that gives your body all the nutrition it needs.

week 9

day 4

WHAT YOU EAT: Fasting

Should people fast? What are the biblical and scientific principles behind fasting, and how should it be done?

Jesus, when confronted as to why his disciples didn't fast, made it clear that a time to fast would come: "But the time will come when the bridegroom will be taken from them; in those days they will fast" (Luke 5:35).

In addition, there has been scientific study that indicates that short fasts of a day or so can be beneficial to the body for detoxifying and cleansing purposes. Also, there is a long precedent in many religions, including Christianity, of the value of using a time of fasting as a means to reconnect with our Creator.

Since the Center has long dealt with both extremes of eating disorders, I always advise caution when considering fasting (if you are concerned, take our online eating-disorder test at www.aplaceofhope.com). Many people who obsess about weight deprive themselves of food to the point of illness and even death. If you have any reason to suspect you might have a tendency toward bulimia or anorexia, you should not fast.

However, in moderation, studies show that occasional short fasts can help to detoxify and cleanse the body. Remember, however, that you should continue to drink your normal requirement of water during a fast day. This helps to accelerate the detoxification and maintain your hydration. It will also help to reduce the hunger you may feel. You should also take a good multivitamin to keep nutrients flowing into your body.

Another thing to watch for is bingeing the day after a fast. If after a day of fasting, you eat two days' worth of food, you would be better off continuing to eat and pray in a consistent manner.

week 9
d a y 5

THE JOURNEY JOURNAL: Sharing with Friends

You're going to like your journal assignments this week (well, at least one of them!).

ASSIGNMENT #1: MAKE A TRIP TO A FAVORITE LOCAL RESTAURANT.

Head out with friends or family to an eating place of your choice. Your mission is to find things on the menu to eat that follow the AWE guidelines but still leave you satisfied. Here are ten tips to help you along.

1. Broth-based soups and salads are always a good choice.
2. Vegetable and chicken quesadillas (if they aren't deep fried) are usually good.
3. Use trips to restaurants to get the fish meals you can't seem to fix at home (broiled or grilled, not deep fried!).
4. If you just can't resist a small steak, talk a friend into splitting it with you, and top it off with a salad or soup.
5. Pocket sandwiches and Greek sandwiches (gyros) can be a good choice.
6. Look for menu selections marked as being "healthy" or "heart friendly" (but still ask questions!).
7. Do your research before going out. For a great

resource, log on to www.dietfacts.com and click on the restaurants link. Here you can find information on thousands of menu items from over a hundred popular restaurants. Make your selection before you ever enter the restaurant, and stick to it.

8. Choose vegetables over meat, fish over chicken, lean meat over red meat.

9. Choose olive oil over vegetable oil, vegetable oil over butter.

10. Deep fried bad, deep fried evil, no eat deep fried! (Is that pointed enough?)

Of course, your choice of restaurant has a lot to do with how hard your selection will be. It's easier to find healthy selections at restaurants that make it a point to cater to a healthy lifestyle.

Healthy eating doesn't mean banishment from restaurants. It just means you have to make smart, informed choices based on what you have learned in this program and not choose your foods impulsively.

WORKSHEET: Restaurant Report

I went to . . .

_____

_____

The following people went with me . . .

_____

_____

I normally would have had . . .

_____

_____

_____

This time I had . . .

_____

_____

From this experience I learned . . .

_____

_____

_____

_____

_____

ASSIGNMENT #2: GIVE A TALK TO YOUR FRIENDS ABOUT WEIGHT LOSS.

This one might be a lot harder, but you can do it! I want you to offer to do a talk for your church group or a group of friends about weight loss. It doesn't have to be a big, formal discussion. If there has been interest in forming a weight-loss group, offer to chair the first meeting. Or organize a "fit and faithful" meeting of your own and invite others to join. Another idea: If your group is going well, offer to go to another church to help them get started. Just pick one chapter to talk about, or give an overview. Passing on the good news keeps you moving toward your goals (which is why we'll talk about it even more in later chapters!). For now, take the plunge—offer your services to get the ball rolling for your friends, church family, or others.

week 9
d a y   6

MAKE IT REAL: Target Exercise

If you have been walking or doing other exercises of choice, you should now be seeing the results. (If you haven't been exercising, *start now!*) However, you may be finding problem areas that just won't go away. If so, it might be time to consider exercises to help you tone those specific areas.

There are tons of books, and as many infomercials, that tell you how to tone your abs, glutes, etc. However, as long as you are in relatively good health (no back problems, etc.), you should be able to target those areas with simple exercise. (As always, check with your doctor before beginning any exercise program.)

Simple exercises, like sit-ups and leg lifts, are really all that are needed to tone your body. Consider the example of Herschel Walker. Walker was a skinny young boy of modest means in Georgia. He had never been into sports, but at age twelve, he asked a youth football coach what he should do to get in shape to play football. "Sit-ups, push-ups, and sprints," the coach told him. Walker took it to heart. Over the next year, he did 100,000 push-ups, 100,000 sit-ups, and sprinted thousands of miles.

Without ever touching a weight, Herschel went on to become the greatest running back in Georgia's history, setting a freshmen running record. He later became an All-Pro NFL player. He was also a world-class track athlete, running stride for stride with track specialists who weighed 60 pounds less than he did.[3]

For much of his career, Walker's only exercise "tool" was his body.

There are a ton of exercise videos, books, etc., on the market to help you target whatever you need to target. If you find these helpful, use them. As always, whatever works for you is best. However, for most of us, all we need is a little knowledge, a little ambition, and the bodies God gave us.

week 9
d a y 7

A VOICE ALONG THE PATH: Kale's Story

I finally got serious about exercising this week.

I had been eating pretty well, and the weight loss was pleasing. However, I hadn't made the commitment to really get into an exercise routine. I was taking my "walks with God" often, but not regularly enough.

However, this week, as I was taking a walk, I passed the Pattersons out for their evening stroll. Mr. and Mrs. Patterson must be almost ninety, but every evening they go out and take a short walk, hand in hand. If it's raining, they take an umbrella. If it's cold, they bundle up. The only time I don't see them out is when there is snow on the sidewalk or there is a thunderstorm or something. They are always out working in their garden as well.

We walked together and chatted for a few moments. They are always cheerful and never complain, even though I know Mrs. Patterson suffers from osteoporosis and walks with a slight limp. As pleasant as the chat was, I didn't feel happy when we parted.

I felt ashamed.

Here I was complaining and whining, if only to myself, about getting out and walking. And I haven't even been conscientious about it. The Pattersons had every good excuse you could think of to sit back on the couch, but they looked upon their evening walks as one of the highlights of their day. They saw it as a chance to be outside, see God's handiwork, and to be with each other and Him.

I took another turn around the block, but this time I looked around me. I observed more than forty varieties of flowers and at least a half-dozen types of trees. The sun, the birds, the grass—and yes, the people—all testimonies to God's creation. There are miracles and grandeur in each step . . . when you bother to see them. And I hadn't been bothering.

I asked God's forgiveness for my blindness and my self-centered attitude. I had had some pleasing results from what I now had to admit was a halfhearted effort. If I showed one-tenth of the perseverance and fortitude the Pattersons showed in their faithful evening walks, what could I do? What could I become?

As I see it, the limits lie only within me.

I turned toward home. Some members of the church had asked me about forming a weight group, and I had been putting them off. I was afraid I would fail. That I might trip up. That people would see me as a hypocrite if I hadn't lost all the weight I intended to. Now I realize that I had been avoiding a chance to serve God because I might fail. I also saw that if I waited for a chance to serve God that didn't involve a risk, I'd still be waiting when I was as old as the Pattersons.

I had some phone calls to make.

the total temple makeover

And hope does not disappoint us, because God has poured out his love into our hearts by the Holy Spirit, whom he has given us.

—Romans 5:5

LIVING WITH GOD, LIVING WITH HOPE!
week 10
day 1

INSPIRATION: Be Still

How often do we take the time to simply be still?

In his "Spiritual Exercises," Saint Ignatius of Loyola outlines a series of exercises to help those who seek a better and more powerful relationship with God. We won't go into detail about the exercises here; if you're interested in further information, go to your public library. But we want to make use of one of his principles to gain understanding of God's will for us: simply be still.

This week I have an activity I want you to do every day. Sometime during each day, go off by yourself for fifteen minutes. No TV, no distractions. Unplug the phone if necessary. Take several deep-cleansing breaths, exhale slowly, and think about where you are in this process. Think about where you need to go, and simply ask God to speak to your heart and mind about what you need to do.

Immediately after those fifteen minutes, record your thoughts and feelings in your journal. Do this each day, and then summarize what you have learned about yourself at the end of the week.

I think you will be amazed.

week 10
d a y 2

DEVOTIONAL: Adding to Your Faith
WHAT'S ON YOUR FRIDGE?

> Make every effort to add to your faith goodness; and to goodness, knowledge; and to knowledge, self-control; and to self-control, perseverance; and to perseverance, godliness; and to godliness, brotherly kindness; and to brotherly kindness, love. For if you possess these qualities in increasing measure, they will keep you from being ineffective and unproductive in your knowledge of our Lord Jesus Christ. (2 Peter 1:5–9)

This week ask God to help you—through intervention, friends, family members, or fellow Christians—to add to your faith those traits that not only make your health better, but *you* better.

Dearest Heavenly Father,

My prayer this week is that You add to my faith. Help me to grow in Your ways and Your will; help me grow in health and fitness; help me grow in strength and persistence. Give me a heart that seeks Your desires; give me a mind that seeks Your purpose for me; give me a spirit that is strong and purposeful; give me a soul that seeks out Your light. Surround me with those who can teach me, help me, support and guide me. Let me receive from them and give to them as needed. And, as always, let me do all things to Your greater glory. Amen.

10

week 10

d a y 3

THOUGHTS FOR FOOD: Metabolism

Over the course of your life, your dietary needs change greatly. Some unknown humorist understood the issue of metabolism well: "The older you get, the tougher it is to lose weight, because by then your body and your fat are really good friends."

When you were born, your metabolic demands were high. Simply growing demanded an immense amount of energy, and from birth to midteens, your body was constantly growing. This was a critical time for most of us, because it was during this time that our eating habits were generally formed. It was also during this time that the consequences of poor eating habits were generally invisible to us. To put it simply, it used to be that children didn't pay as great a price for eating poorly in terms of gaining weight. However, times are changing. Now childhood obesity is becoming an explosive health problem, much like adult obesity. Our sedate lifestyles, along with poor eating habits, are catching up to us all, young and old alike.

As you get older, your metabolic rate naturally tends to slow down, as your body does not have to support the growth cycle. Unfortunately, we tend to continue to eat as we did when we were younger. Usually around this time, many of us get married, and our eating habits undergo another large change as we learn to adapt to living with another person. A study done by the North American Association for the Study of Obesity found that the first two years of marriage saw a significant increase in participants' Body Mass Index (BMI). In short, consumption goes up, and activity goes down.

As we progress into middle age and beyond, our bodies continue to change. The muscle mass in our tissue becomes "marbled" with fat, our bone density decreases, and our energy levels go down.

However, the effects of time are not inevitable. Today—right now— you can begin to prepare your body for the years ahead, no matter what age you are. Here are some general tips for different age groups:

Kids (3–12)

Introduce kids to soy milk as an alternative to dairy products. Get them to enjoy yogurt with fruit more than fatty ice creams. Get them on the water kick rather than the soda kick. *Now* is when you have a huge influence over their choices, so help them choose wisely.

Teens (13–19)

The battle with this age group will be against junk foods. As teens grow in independence, they eat fewer and fewer meals at home. Make sure the meals you do control are healthy, and take the time to talk to your kids about nutrition. We warn kids about the dangers of drugs and smoking, but we need to do the same thing with obesity.

By the way, concerning smoking, I think its relationship to health and weight loss was best summed up by a bumper sticker I once saw: *"Smoking helps you lose weight—one lung at a time!"*

Young Adult (20–40)

This is the critical time of transition for most of us, and the time period where many lose the battle of weight. It's important to work toward ever-better eating habits and ever-greater levels of activity to avoid falling into the middle-age bulge trap.

10

Golden Years (40+)

As the body cycles begin to wind down, we need to adapt our eating and exercise with it. Calcium from foods like yogurt and soy should play a larger role in our diets, and we need to adapt our exercise to incorporate more aerobic and fewer high-impact activities. In addition, those who might be at risk for diseases such as Alzheimer's will want to include rich sources of Omega-3 and antioxidants in their diet. There is a huge amount of data that suggests mental acuity in older individuals can be directly related to diet. That means we have the power to reduce the effects of age on our minds. And, equally important, a poor diet can increase our risk.

Change Your Habits!

New Habit #10: Adjust the amount and type of foods you eat to suit your age.

Healthy eating truly is a life-changing experience. God wants each day you spend on this earth to be fruitful, abundant, and joyful. Do your part by making sure your body is prepared for every stage of life. No matter what age you are, take those baby steps necessary for building joy and success!

week 10
d a y 4

WHAT YOU EAT: Beverages

One form of food we haven't talked about specifically (except for water) is beverages. Of course, beverages like fruit juices, etc., are also included in the proper food groups we have already discussed. But now it's time to directly address the question of beverage choices and how they can help or hurt your weight loss.

A good resource to check out different beverages and drinks is www.bevnet.com—a review network that gives nutritional information on beverages similar to the way www.dietfacts.com reviews restaurants.

One note before we examine different types of beverages: the best way to get plenty of fluids is to eat a diet rich in vegetables and fruits. Why is that? Because vegetables and fruits are great sources of pure, fresh water. A large serving of watermelon will be filling, delicious, and provide excellent quantities of fluids. So don't neglect the "high-water" foods. If you leave the table after a meal feeling thirsty, it is a good indicator you need more liquid in your foods.

Now let's look at the different choices of beverages, and make some informed decisions on how to choose them wisely.

+ *Water.* You knew this was coming. You need to drink a minimum of 32 ounces of water per day; 64 ounces of water per day will do more to promote weight loss.

- *Juices.* After pure water, the next best choice is a pure fruit juice. If you have a juicer tucked back somewhere, now would be a great time to dust it off and start making your own juices again. Keep in mind that some of the nutrients and fiber are lost when fruit is squeezed to make juice, and many manufactured juices contain added sweeteners and are high in calories, so you would do better to eat a serving of fruit accompanied with a glass of water, instead.

- *Flavored waters.* Most flavored waters contain sugars—normally fructose. Although fructose is preferable to sucrose in terms of the Glycemic Load, flavored waters should be considered just a "change of pace" drink for occasional consumption. Choose those with natural juices for flavoring over those with artificial flavors.

- *Coffee.* As we all know, coffee contains caffeine—a stimulant. The debate has been going back and forth for years over the negatives versus the positives of coffee. I drink coffee; I like it. The key here is moderation. If you enjoy a cup or two of coffee during the day, then go ahead—just don't make it ten! And remember that caffeine is a diuretic, so you'll need to replace the fluids lost with water to counteract the diuretic effect.

- *Wine/alcohol.* In recent years much has been made of the health benefits of a glass of wine each day. Red wine contains *resveratrol*, a form of phytoestrogen believed to promote cardiovascular health, which is concentrated in the skin of the grape. Since grape skins are removed earlier in the production of white wines, resveratrol is more prevalent in red wine. However, it should be noted that the same levels of resveratrol and antioxidants could be derived from pure grape juice as well as red wine. Other forms of alcohol show relatively little health benefits when you consider the health risks of their abuse.

- *Teas.* The same cautions against caffeine in coffee apply to black teas. However, green teas can offer a variety of benefits for health and weight loss. For one thing, like grapes, green teas are a source of phytoestrogens, a plant-based estrogen that can help improve bone density. Green teas are also rich sources of antioxidants, which can help reduce the risk of certain forms of cancer. Finally, green teas are generally much lower in caffeine than black tea. A cup of green tea in the middle of the day can provide a moment of repose and tranquility to help reduce stress levels, so consider following the British tradition by having a daily tea time in your schedule.

- *Soft drinks.* Most soft drinks should be consumed in moderation (my preference is none), certainly no more than one per day. Avoid caffeinated, high-sugar drinks in favor of low-sugar, lemon-lime choices. By all means, don't get your children on the concentrated sugar habit. Encourage them toward water, and they will thank you years from now. There is growing evidence that we can form an addiction to sugar, much as people do to drugs and alcohol. So don't put that burden on your children! What about diet sodas? Diet sodas contain aspartame, an artificial sweetener and one I don't recommend. In addition, most diet sodas contain caffeine, a diuretic, which means you should drink even more water to compensate. I've just heard too many accounts of people who have become "addicted" to their diet sodas, drinking far too many during the day and far too little water.

AWE: Beverages		
avoid	watch	eat
High-sugar soft drinks	Coffee	Pure water
Alcohol	Black tea	Green teas
Diet sodas	Wine	
	Flavored water	
	Fruit juices	

Figure 19.

week 10

d a y 5

THE JOURNEY JOURNAL: Stretch Your Mind and Spirit

How can you grow in your relationship with our Father? Just try these exercises! (And don't worry; these are relatively easy.)

- ◆ View a religious-based movie you have not watched before with your family. Write about the movie in your journal, and talk about the things you learned that could apply to your Christian life. (Some suggested titles: *The Mission, The Cross and the Switchblade, Messiah, The Hope,* and *The Passion of the Christ.* For a list of movies from a Christian perspective, visit www.praize.com.)

- ◆ Read a book about the life and times of Jesus. It's important to understand not only the words of the Bible but the context of the world in which they were written. I recommend *The Jesus I Never Knew* by Philip Yancey, but check with your pastor as well for book and movie recommendations. Write about the book in your journal, or make notes as you read.

- ◆ Pick one city or region from the Bible and try to learn what it was like in Jesus's time. What were the main businesses? What was the ethnic makeup of the people?

Who were their leaders and rulers? How did the Roman rule influence the daily life of Christians? Put a human face on some of the stories of the Bible, and you will find yourself growing in your faith. Record your observations in your journal.

week 10
d a y 6

MAKE IT REAL: Qualities for Success

How do you develop the qualities needed for success?

We may long to succeed both spiritually and physically, yet are clueless how to proceed.

Sometimes, even with our best efforts to grow spiritually, we become distracted by life issues that seem to remain the same. No matter how much we desire to change them, we are left with a longing to fill a void inside and to find the answers for so many things that do not seem to have answers. If we don't find a spiritual answer, we often travel down a path in search of physical substitutes to fill that void, rather than finding the answer through increased strength and depth in our spiritual walk.[1]

The spiritual path each of us walks is different, of course. I cannot know where you are on yours or the strength of your faith as you read these words. But it is my wish and hope that your faith has progressed with your improving health.

In this chapter I'll discuss directly the connection between spiritual health and physical health. To begin, read this excerpt from a fellow traveler.

> Janet, a friend, had told me about this great new weight-loss program she had found. I had seen the positive changes in her, so I

thought I would try it. At first it was great; I started seeing some real progress in myself. After a while, though, I started finding excuses to miss meetings. I didn't stay as involved with the activities as I had when I started out. The positive changes that had come so quickly at first started to slow down and even started going backward. After a while I just got tired of it and stopped going. Today I find myself pretty much back where I started . . . just a little more disillusioned.

A common enough occurrence, you might think. Now read the paragraph below, about someone like you struggling in his or her Christian relationship.

Janet, a friend, had told me about this great new church she had found. I had seen the positive changes in her, so I thought I would try it. At first it was great; I started seeing some real progress in myself. After a while, though, I started finding excuses to miss services. I didn't stay as involved with the activities as I had when I started out. The positive changes that had come so quickly at first started to slow down and even started going backward. After a while I just got tired of it and stopped going. Today I find myself pretty much back where I started . . . just a little more disillusioned.

What's my point in having you read essentially the same text twice? To show that the same qualities needed for successful weight loss are the same qualities needed for your spiritual walk. Things like persistence, self-motivation, the courage to take risks, and self-confidence aren't merely necessary tools to lose a few pounds; they are necessary tools to gain a new life. These are not gifts you either have or don't have; they are skills you learn by taking those baby steps and earning small victories each day. If you want to think of them as gifts, then they are gifts that lie within *each* of us, if we will allow them to flourish.

week 10

d a y 7

A VOICE ALONG THE PATH: Notes from Kale's "Be Still" Exercises

Day 1

I don't know that I learned a lot new. I didn't really hear anything. It was surprising how hard it was to just stay still, with my eyes closed, for fifteen minutes. It seemed like an eternity, and I thought I was going to nod off. It was a little hard to do the breathing and clear my mind, but after a while, the timing became natural, and I stopped counting.

I have to admit, I felt more relaxed.

Day 3

I'm beginning to understand how this exercise is supposed to help. The first two days I kept trying to force something to happen. Then tonight I really felt like the way to handle a problem I am wrestling with just came to me. Like it came from outside me. Was it God speaking to me? He made my heart, He made my mind, so if my mind creates a solution, is that a message from God? Hmmm . . . something to think about tomorrow night.

Day 4

I bought some earplugs, like they use in factories. My neighbor's dog kept barking at night, and it was keeping me from really focusing. The weird thing was, when I put them in, it was amazing how enclosed I felt. I could hear my heartbeats, my breathing, all the things going on in my body. No breakthroughs tonight, but it definitely feels like I'm making progress.

Day 6

I hadn't noticed it, but I have slept soundly for four nights straight! Usually I'm an "up and down" type of person. However, I have slept straight through, and I seem to be getting up more alert. It's amazing what the proper type and amount of sleep will do for you!

Day 7

I've decided I really like this quiet time, I'm going to make it a permanent part of my routine. I use it to review my day, think of the mistakes I made, ask God to forgive them, and then ask Him to help me let them go. I also ask Him to help me forgive the wrongs that may have been done to me during the day. I'm not sure if and how it helps me to lose weight, but I sure go to bed with my heart feeling lighter!

the total temple makeover

The LORD will indeed give what is good, and our land will yield its harvest.

—Psalm 85:12

REAPING THE HARVEST
week 11
d a y 1

INSPIRATION: Making a Difference

Can you believe it's week eleven of our program?

By now your new eating habits, your exercise program, and your Christian mind-set should be in place. So it's time to start thinking about spreading the results of your work and God's grace throughout the world.

That's right, I said throughout the world. I don't know your situation as you read this. You may be in financial distress, you may be suffering from or recovering from abuse, or you may feel totally inadequate to such a task.

If so, take a moment to read this poignant story.

The Legend of the Starfish

A vacationing businessman was walking along a beach when he saw a young boy. Along the shore were many starfish that had been washed up by the tide and were sure to die before the tide returned.

The boy walked slowly along the shore and occasionally reached down and tossed the beached starfish back into the ocean.

The businessman, hoping to teach the boy a little lesson in common sense, walked up to the boy and said, "I have been watching what you are doing, son. You have a good heart, and I know you mean well, but do you realize how many beaches there are around here and how many starfish are dying on every beach every day? Surely such an industrious and kind-hearted boy such as yourself could find something better to do with your time. Do you really think that what you are doing is going to make a difference?"

The boy looked up at the man, and then he looked down at a starfish by his feet. He picked up the starfish, and as he gently tossed it back into the ocean, he said, "It makes a difference to that one."[1]

We all know the story of Jesus's ministry. Imagine yourself as one of the seventy disciples, gathered together after the Ascension. You look into each others' eyes. You have been given a charge by the Teacher to spread His word to every corner of the globe. You look over the ragtag band assembled there—no great wealth, no political power, many are not even gifted speakers. A single legion of the Roman army could decimate the entire band in minutes, and this motley group is supposed to change the world? Impossible!

Yet here you and I are, two thousand years later, talking about Jesus's life and the difference He has made to us. I think that small band would be amazed at all that has grown from what they accomplished. I also think they would, without hesitation, point out, "There is still so much that can be done."

So much that can be done.

I have known people who have taken on very difficult challenges in life, such as doing mission work in far-off countries, being a foster parent to a special-needs child, or providing hospice care to those facing their last days on earth. The amazing thing is, no matter how hard or emotionally wrenching the task, I have never heard anyone say that they regretted getting involved. In fact, each and every one has talked about what they received from their activities, not what they gave up.

You may already be involved in some projects. If so, God bless you! Then look for ways to get more involved, do bigger and better things, and fulfill even more exciting dreams. Our exercise this week will help you focus your desires and energies in a fruitful direction.

One of the best ways you can contribute might be to help others struggling with the dual issues of weight and faith. Most recovery programs require that clients help someone else who is just beginning the process. The reason? It strengthens both the new person and the person giving the assistance.

This week I challenge you to make a difference in the world . . . one little starfish at a time.

week 11
d a y   2

DEVOTIONAL: Reaching Out

WHAT'S ON YOUR FRIDGE?

> Do not withhold good from those who deserve it,
> when it is in your power to act. (Proverbs 3:27)

Focus on helping someone start down the path you have walked, and in doing so, find strength for your own continuing journey.

This week pray for *power*!

Most Mighty and Gracious God,

I am Yours to use as You see fit. As the potter shapes the vessel, make me into Your tool to do Your bidding this day. Give me the wisdom to know Your desires for me. Give me the courage to walk the path You place before me. And give me the power to do the good on this earth You would have me do. Let me not turn away from the pain of my brothers and sisters, but do not let it bring despair. Let me see the need, and meet it. Let me hear the cry, and answer it. Let me feel the pain, and comfort it. I ask for the power to do these things, so that all might know Your power and grace. As all good things flow from You, let the glory and honor be Yours. In Christ's name I pray, Amen.

week 11

d a y 3

THOUGHTS FOR FOOD: Meal Plans

Now that we have laid the groundwork for proper food choices, it's time to start putting those ideas in place.

CHANGE YOUR HABITS!

New Habit #11: Plan your meals.

In this section I'll outline a weekly meal plan that you can adapt to your own needs.

A WEEKLY MEAL PLANNER

I know that in most weight-loss books the weekly planner comes very early, usually in the first chapter. However, it has been my experience that few, if any, actually do a meal plan for the week. At best, they do it diligently for two or three weeks and then start to taper off. So, even though I've included a blank Weekly Meal Planner in appendix G for you to copy and use, it is the *daily* meal outline that I consider most important, since it will guide you in meal decisions even when you are making them at the last moment. And it's concise enough to write on a 3 x 5 card and carry with you. You can make a new card at the start of every day. Or you can copy the Planner in appendix H. The example on the following page shows you how it looks.

Daily Meal Planner	
Breakfast	
Midmorning Snack	
Lunch	
Afternoon Snack	
Dinner	
End of the Day Treat	

Figure 20.

Let's look at some of the basic principles of the outline.

Breakfast

It may sound like a 1960s TV commercial, but there is solid research that shows that eating a morning meal is not only important for energy, but also for weight loss. A study conducted on obese men found that those who did not eat anything in the morning tended to overeat more later in the day—actually consuming more total calories than those who ate a healthy breakfast. If you think of it in terms of the Glycemic Load, skipping breakfast after sleeping all night forces a sharp drop in the blood-sugar levels, and this results in feeling famished, which causes us to eat more of the wrong things later in the day. So a good, solid breakfast is important to healthy eating.

Midmorning Snack

Evidence suggests that eating certain foods at different times may aid digestion, and it's a good idea to hold off on the fruits and eat one serving as a midmorning snack. An apple, plum, or nectarine should give you a nice boost to enter lunchtime not feeling too hungry. If you can split a serving into a couple of minisnacks between breakfast and lunch, so much the better. Also, don't forget to drink eight ounces of water a half hour or so before lunch to help reduce hunger.

Lunch

Your lunch should include a serving of protein and should be rich in nonstarchy vegetables. If your family is not that keen on fish, use this time when most family members are on their own for lunch to get a serving of fish into your meal. A filling and delicious meal could include a tuna or chicken salad or a serving of tuna with a side of green beans and a side salad topped off with a fruit cup or a serving of watermelon, etc. Ideally, lunch should be your big meal of the day, in terms of calories. Eating late at night works against weight loss. If you have an hour for lunch, try to work in a fifteen-minute walk before eating. Such moderate exercise will not only burn calories but also reduce your hunger cravings.

Afternoon Snack

Have a sugar-free pudding cup, lite yogurt, etc., and a cup of green tea for your tea time.

Again, don't forget to get in at least eight ounces of water before your snack, as well as before the evening meal.

Dinner

Your evening meal should consist of a protein, green vegetables, some grains, and a light dessert. An example meal would be wheat spaghetti with tomato sauce, ground turkey, spices, and Parmesan cheese sprinkled lightly on top, with a side dish of zucchini, lightly grilled in garlic and olive oil, a small side salad, and gelatin with light whipped cream for dessert.

11

End of the Day Treat

End your day with a treat—either cinnamon herbal tea or sugar-free decaffeinated cocoa—to help you prepare for a restful night. Add a graham cracker or another low-fat cracker if you wish. I find that teas that contain valerian, St. John's Wort, and echinacea help me rest well at night, though that is a personal observation.

Daily meals like the ones outlined here will help you feel full and satisfied, while still moving you forward toward your weight goals.

Have a special recipe you would like to share with us? E-mail it to mystory@aplaceofhope.com.

week 11
d a y 4

WHAT YOU EAT: Snacks

We've touched on snacks in other chapters, but since the snack foods you choose can have such a devastating effect on any weight-loss effort, I want to talk specifically about how to make them work for you in your weight-loss efforts, rather than being the "lard landmines" they can become.

Obviously we have a lot of options in this country when it comes to snacks. In 2001 the sales of sugar and confectionary products alone were $36 billion; soft drinks were another $76 billion. The average American consumes more than 170 pounds of refined sugar a year, and the figure continues to increase. In 1987 soda consumption surpassed water consumption for the first time.

THE SNACK ATTACK

We all know what we should be eating for a quick bite, but the temptation to "treat" ourselves is often too great. The battle begins at the grocery store, where we pick out the foods we wish to snack on. It continues in the kitchen, where we decide to prepare healthy snacks ahead of time, rather than waiting until the "attack" occurs. It ends in our mind, where we decide how and when we will feed the occasional craving.

Some researchers feel that sugar craving approaches being a true addiction, with many of the same symptoms. In a study at Princeton in 2002, for example, Dr. Bartley Hoebel demonstrated that rats "hooked" on sugar go through withdrawal symptoms and continue to crave sweets for weeks afterward.[2]

Just as bad, of course, are high-fat snacks, like potato chips and pork rinds, beef jerky (which contains an extremely high amount of sodium), and crackers that tend to contain a great deal of trans-fats. The rule on snack foods has to be: read the label.

So, what should we do to counterattack the traditional snack? Here is a summarized AWE list for snacks (some may have already appeared in previous charts).

AWE: Snacks		
avoid	**watch**	**eat**
High-sugar soft drinks	Sherbets	Frozen grapes and berries
Packaged sweets	Low-fat ice creams	
		Lite yogurts
Fried chips, etc.	"Energy" bars	
		Sugar-free pudding (Pudding Pops)
Chocolate and candy bars	Fruit juices (frozen fruit-juice pops)	
Cookies		A bowl of high-grain cereal
	Baked chips	
Diets sodas		
Cakes and pastries		

Figure 21.

week 11

d a y 5

THE JOURNEY JOURNAL: A One-Week Practice Plan

Your journal assignment is to prepare a week's worth of meals and snacks using the form provided in appendix G, Weekly Meal Planner.

As I said earlier, I have no illusions that you will do a weekly plan for the rest of your life. If you do have the discipline and will to do so, wonderful. Feel free to make use of this tool. However, if you go through the exercise even one time, you'll feel confident in where and how to find the recipes you need to continue eating better.

Make a copy of the sheet, and take it to the library or get on the Internet. Look for books or Web pages with low Glycemic Index recipes for diabetics. For example, using the Google search engine, I found 10,500 Web pages using the terms "recipes healthy glycemic."

Now begin looking for recipes you can use for different meals.

For example, on the next page is a recipe for a snack item—Spicy Pita Chips—that I found on the Web site www.naturalhealthdoc.net:[3]

Spicy Pita Chips

Ingredients
4 whole-wheat pita bread rounds
butter-flavored cooking spray
1 teaspoon garlic powder
1/2 teaspoon paprika
1/4 teaspoon ground red pepper

Instructions
1. Split each pita bread round into 2 rounds.
2. Spray the rough side with butter-flavored cooking spray.
3. Combine remaining ingredients and sprinkle evenly over pita breads.
4. Cut each round into 8 wedges (use a pizza wheel cutter).
5. Place wedges on a baking sheet coated with cooking spray.
6. Bake at 300 degrees for 20 minutes or until lightly browned and crisp. Yield: 64 chips.
7. Store in an airtight container for up to 1 week.

Note from Dr. Jantz: to further improve this recipe, you might substitute Olivio spread or olive oil as the spray.

Here is another from the same site that could be a breakfast dish. It's a wonderful baked egg dish for any time of the day. Call it Pizza Eggs, and the kids will love it.

Shirred Egg Supreme

Ingredients
1/2 teaspoon softened butter
4 tablespoons tomato sauce, pizza sauce, or spaghetti sauce
1 small slice mozzarella cheese
1 egg salt and pepper to taste
1 teaspoon grated Parmesan cheese

Instructions
1. Preheat the oven to 350 degrees.
2. Butter an individual-size baking dish or large custard cup.

3. Place 2 tablespoons sauce in dish.
4. Add mozzarella cheese.
5. Carefully break the egg into the dish.
6. Season with salt and pepper.
7. Top with remaining 2 tablespoons sauce, and sprinkle with Parmesan.
8. Bake for about 12–15 minutes, until eggs are set. The white will be cooked; the yolk will be liquid, like a soft-boiled egg.

Yield: 1 serving.

Note from Dr. Jantz: Again, I would substitute Olivio or another trans-fat-free spread for the butter. If you are concerned about cholesterol, you can use an egg substitute or just the egg whites. You can also use vegetarian cheese substitutes for the cheeses if you wish, but I prefer to use the real thing and just go lightly. If you substitute salsa for the pizza sauce, you have a Western omelet–style dish; with a few more spices you can have a Southwestern style dish as well.

OK, you get the idea. Take the Weekly Meal Planner chart in appendix G and find dishes for each meal on the chart. By the time you are done, you will begin to see how you can make this new diet plan both fun and relatively easy to adopt. Feel free to change the recipes you find to match what you have learned in this book, and try some of them out on your family and friends next week!

11

week 11
d a y 6

MAKE IT REAL: Mental Gymnastics

Make time for play! And this time it's a different kind of gymnastics—mental gymnastics.

I've talked a lot about the body and spirit in this book, but one area of health that cannot be neglected is the mind. As I've pointed out, certain foods (especially those rich in Omega-3 fatty acids, such as fish) assist in keeping the mental processes sharp. Studies from the *New England Journal of Medicine* and Penn State University also show that the best way to keep your mind sharp is to use it!

Just as the explosion of TV and video games has led to a more sedentary lifestyle, so, too, have our minds become soft. We don't challenge ourselves enough mentally anymore. You, of course, might be the exception, but it can't hurt to increase your mental stimulation.

GET YOUR BRAIN IN TRAINING!

Here are some ideas to get your brain back in training this week:

- Sit down and play an old-fashioned board game with friends or family this week.
- Attend a concert, movie, play, etc., that you would normally never consider. Learn about a different art form.
- Try some art or a craft that you have always wanted to do,

but never attempted, such as sculpting or writing poetry. It doesn't matter how good it is. What matters is how good it makes you feel to experience new things.

◆ Write some letters this week—real handwritten letters—to some friends you haven't talked to in a long time. Tell them about your life, tell them about your weight loss, and remind them of their importance to you.

◆ Sponsor a "games night" at church; it's a great way to learn more about your brothers and sisters from your church family.

◆ Go to the library, pick a book at random, and read it all the way through.

◆ Learn to play cribbage, bridge, backgammon, or some other game you don't know much about.

◆ Take a lesson on a musical instrument you've always wanted to learn to play.

◆ Work crosswords, puzzles, or mental games. There are a ton of books and Web sites available to test your mind.

◆ Attend a recital or a lecture on a subject new to you.

◆ Take a drive and explore a town nearby that you have never spent time in before. Stop by the library and town hall and ask about its history, including any unique places to visit, etc.

◆ Visit a different church this Sunday.

week 11
d a y 7

A VOICE ALONG THE PATH: Kale's Story

I went bowling this week!

I've never been one to bowl, but I have to admit, it was a hoot. Of course, I wasn't very good, but I was too busy laughing to notice or care. I haven't laughed that much in a long time. It felt good.

Let's see what else? I fixed a dinner for my fellow "fit and faithful" members this week, and I have to say it was pretty good. The dessert was so-so, but everything else was great, and everyone asked for the recipes. All in all, pretty successful.

I also signed up to take a sign-language course. We have a child in our church who is deaf, and I think it would be nice if she could communicate with somebody else besides her parents, even if I just learn a few common phrases.

I just read back over this week's entries, and I can't believe it's me writing them! I was the person who never left the house, hardly. I didn't go out; I certainly didn't go bowling, and I tried to avoid crowds.

It's almost like I'm a different person.

I've been thinking about the story of Lazarus this week—how Jesus called him up out of that tomb, out of death, and back into the light of day.

I think I understand how he felt. It's as though my life has been given back to me, refreshed and renewed—all because I turned it over to our Lord.

And the Lord knows I haven't been perfect during this process. I've eaten things I shouldn't have; I've sat when I should have exercised; I've indulged in self-pity when I should have been praying for strength. Still, I never completely gave up. I never let those demons pull me back down all the way; I kept fighting forward. And somewhere along the way, I'm not quite sure where, I crossed over to a new horizon.

I'm tired, so I'll go to bed now. But it's a good tired, a fatigue of accomplishment, not despair. And unlike before, I can't wait to get up in the morning.

Each dawn is truly a new day for me now.

the total temple makeover

For the Mighty One has done great things for me—
Holy is his name.

—Luke 1:49

TRANSFORMATION– REBORN

week 12

d a y   1

INSPIRATION: A New Creature in Christ

Welcome and congratulations, you are a new creature in Christ! "Therefore, if anyone is in Christ, he is a new creation; the old has gone, the new has come!" (2 Corinthians 5:17).

When we began this journey twelve weeks ago, we made a promise to each other. You promised to learn, to believe, and to try. I promised that if you would do those things, you would become a new creature in Christ. I rejoice with you in all that you have accomplished and for all that is still to come.

You may feel that you have not done everything you set out to do. You may not have achieved every goal you wished, exercised as often as you should have, done all the things outlined in these chapters. Well, guess what? That is all right! Our goal on this journey has been to take those baby steps.

So ask yourself three simple questions.

1. Do I feel better?
2. Am I a better Christian for the experience?
3. Do I have better knowledge of how to live a healthy and spiritual life?

If you answered yes to those questions, you can hardly consider this a failure, can you? This wasn't some college class with a final at the end of the semester. This was a program designed to begin equipping you with the tools and knowledge to live a better life. The only final exam you have to take is the big one—when you are standing before the Father!

But each new day is the chance to become a "new creature" in Christ: "Therefore we do not lose heart. Though outwardly we are wasting away, yet inwardly we are being renewed day by day" (2 Corinthians 4:16).

You are to be congratulated. It is never an easy thing to take a cold, sober assessment of ourselves, to decide what we like and what we do not, and to try and change for the better. It is even harder in a world made cold and dark by pain, suffering, cruelty, and apathy to decide that you will walk the path laid out by Christ on a mountain called Golgotha, all those centuries ago.

Paul tells us we should delight in our good works, for they further the kingdom of God. It is not vanity, or pride, but a simple rejoicing that His will is done. That is what you have been doing over these last twelve weeks.

So this week we'll celebrate, we'll review all that has come before, and we'll discuss some ways that you can go forward from here.

week 12
d a y   2

DEVOTIONAL: GIVE THANKS!
WHAT'S ON YOUR FRIDGE?

> You are the God who performs miracles;
> You display your power among the peoples.
> (Psalm 77:14)

Let's give thanks for the miracles God has worked in your life over the last twelve weeks! Perhaps you don't feel you experienced any miracles, and in the Cecile B. DeMille-parting-of-the-Red-Sea variety, you might be right. However, God's miracles come in all shapes and sizes. Think about the day you walked up the steps without getting winded or the day you made it all the way around the mall in less than fifteen minutes. Or the day you put on those pants that you hadn't worn in a year. These minimiracles are evidence of the life-changing decisions you have made, and you can be certain that God is pleased and proud of you!

Dear God,

You were there in the beginning of all things. You were there in the beginning of my life, and You were there twelve weeks ago when I began this journey. You know my trials and triumphs along the way. Thank You for the successes that give me hope, the failures

12

that teach me humility, and the love of good friends and my brothers and sisters that gives me support. Help me to remember that, even now, I have only begun. There is so much more I can do, so much more I can be, and so much more I can give in Your service. Keep me strong, keep me safe, and keep me moving forward on the path You have set before me. To You goes the thanks, and the praise, and the glory. Amen.

week 12
d a y 3

THOUGHTS FOR FOOD: A Better Pyramid

As you've worked with me through the food pyramid, you've also seen several flaws in its construction. These flaws have become so apparent that the FDA will soon issue a new food pyramid patterned after the one below.[4]

Figure 22.

As you can see, it is very different from the original pyramid used at the beginning of this book. But it follows more closely the principles I've been outlining in this book.

The *foundation* of the pyramid is exercise and weight control. These should always be the basis of a healthy body.

In *level two*, we see whole-meal foods (whole gains), which should be included with every meal. In addition, vegetable oils (unsaturated fats) should be part of almost every meal. Here I deviated to say that olive oil should make up the vast majority of the vegetable oils you use.

Level three consists of vegetables (eaten abundantly) and fruit (two to three portions a day). Again, green, nonstarchy vegetables should be the preference here. Since fruits seem to digest best when taken alone, consider making them the bulk of your snack foods (frozen grapes, fruit ice snacks, etc.).

Level four is nuts and pulses (beans). These provide critical vegetable proteins and should be eaten one to three times a day. Soups, dips, and side dishes are a great way to satisfy the requirements of this food group.

Fish, poultry, and eggs make up *level five* (zero to two portions per day). I would emphasize fish from this group, since the Omega-3 acids are abundant in fresh cold-water fish.

Dairy products and calcium supplements make up *level six*. It's a simple matter to get one to two portions per day from a serving of cheese and a yogurt snack.

The *top level* (seven) is those items that should be eaten sparingly, not more than once or twice a week. These include red meat and butter (high-saturated fat items) in one section and high-carbohydrate foods (white rice, white bread, etc.) in the other. As we know from our reading, high-saturated fats, especially trans-fats, have a bad effect on the metabolism and the functioning of the heart. High-starch foods have an extremely high Glycemic Load and lead to high levels of blood sugar.

CHANGE YOUR HABITS!

New Habit #12: Use the new food pyramid as a guide to healthy eating.

If you look at the AWE list for each type of food we discussed, you'll find that the recommendations in this book match this new food pyramid very well. It isn't perfect—no simple guideline like this is—but it goes a long way in addressing some of the problems of the current food pyramid. So make a copy of this pyramid (see appendix I), cut it out, and tape it to your refrigerator. Refer to it when making out your shopping lists and planning your meals—it will provide a good guide to eating healthier.

week 12
d a y 4

WHAT YOU EAT: A Complete Plan for Healthier Eating

In appendix J, we have summarized the AWE chart, so you'll have an easy reference for each major food group. Copy this chart and place it on the fridge next to the new food pyramid. Together, the two will give you a complete game plan for healthier eating.

Always remember that the guidelines are just that—*guidelines*. You won't immediately blow up by five pounds if you happen to eat something that isn't on the approved list. Simply try to stick to the "Eat" foods as much as possible.

week 12
d a y 5

THE JOURNEY JOURNAL: Celebrating Your Progress

Since this week is a celebration of the progress you have made, we'll go easy on the journal work. Read back through your journal, and answer the following questions.

- What things have I learned about myself during these twelve weeks?
- What things have I learned about my faith over the last twelve weeks?
- What was the best thing about the experience?
- What was the worst thing about the experience?
- Am I a better person today? If so, how?
- What do I plan to do from here?

That's it. Take as little or as much space as you need for each question, and take time to reflect on each one before answering. It is important to summarize where you are at this point before moving forward.

week 12
d a y 6

MAKE IT REAL: What Next?

Where do I go from here?

That is the big question, isn't it? Hopefully during the last twelve weeks, you've seen the Lord working great changes in you and for you. Now is the time to decide where your path will take you next.

You basically have two options. If you are unhappy with where you are, with the results you have gotten, then simply turn back to page one and start again. That is not a mark of defeat; it simply means that you have more work to do and that another cycle can be of help. Some people who follow the system may benefit from two or three cycles before they feel in control of their eating and health issues.

If you have been doing this as part of a group, then you should all plan a "graduation." Have a meal, share with each other what you have gained and learned, and make plans to continue to meet or share as you need to maintain your improvements. If you have been following it alone, then have a celebration with family and friends. It's important to celebrate your successes in life. They are milestones marking who you were then, and who you are now—and the "new creature" in Christ you have become is certainly worth celebrating!

Also, if you haven't done so already, it's time to get serious about sharing what you have learned with others. Offer to teach a session at your church, or give a copy of the book to friends and relatives. Talk to kids in your local schools about healthy eating. Offer to go to other churches and help them get groups going. Most of all, continue to grow in mind, body, and spirit. Moving ever forward is critical to continued success. It is when we think we have "made it" and become complacent that we are in the greatest danger of falling back.

Continue working on your new life, and let us know about your achievements by writing us at the Center: mystory@aplaceofhope.com. Tell us what worked, and send us your before and after pictures. *Any* ideas you have are welcome.

Congratulations, great success, and God bless you! With God's help you can do it! "If you can?" said Jesus. "Everything is possible for him who believes" (Mark 9:23).

week 12
d a y 7

A VOICE ALONG THE PATH: Kale's Story

Sundays are my favorite day of the week. We go to church and sit as a family.

Afterward we'll go home and have a light lunch, maybe grill salmon steaks outside. Then we will play volleyball in the yard with our neighbors, go for a walk around the pond, or ride bikes in the park. We'll take a book and sit under a tree while the boys play basketball or ride skateboards. In the evening we'll sit outside and play guitars and sing.

Sometimes I catch a glance of myself in the glass of the French doors. It's hard to believe that it's the same person whose life used to revolve around food. I'm healthier and happier than I've been in a long time. My only regrets are the years I let bad foods and worse thoughts steal away from me. Still, it can't compare to the tomorrows that will come. It seems like all the opportunities of the world are open to me.

And no one calls me fat.

APPENDIX A

BODY MASS INDEX

One of the measurements we want to track is the Body Mass Index (BMI). This index is basically a ratio of height to weight that gives you an indicator of where you need to be to have a healthy weight for your height. To calculate your BMI, do the following:

Write down your weight in pounds   _____

Multiply it by 703   _____

Divide by your height in inches   _____

Divide by your height again   _____

This should be a rough estimate of your BMI. The BMI should fall somewhere between 18 and 50. You can verify the calculation against the chart below:

DETERMINING YOUR BODY MASS INDEX

The following table has already done the math and metric conversions for you. To use the table, find your height in the column on the left. Move across the row to your current weight. The number at the top of the column is the BMI for that height and weight.

BMI (kg/m²)	19	20	21	22	23	24	25	26	27	28	29	30	35	40
HEIGHT (inches)	Weight (pounds)													
58	91	96	100	105	110	115	119	124	129	134	138	143	167	191
59	94	99	104	109	114	119	124	128	133	138	143	148	173	198
60	97	102	107	112	118	123	128	133	138	143	148	153	179	204
61	100	106	111	116	122	127	132	137	143	148	153	158	185	211
62	104	109	115	120	126	131	136	142	147	153	158	164	191	218
63	107	113	118	124	130	135	141	146	152	158	163	169	197	225
64	110	116	122	128	134	140	145	151	157	163	169	174	204	232
65	114	120	126	132	138	144	150	156	162	168	174	180	210	240
66	118	124	130	136	142	148	155	161	167	173	179	186	216	247
67	121	127	134	140	146	153	159	166	172	178	185	191	223	255
68	125	131	138	144	151	158	164	171	177	184	190	197	230	262
69	128	135	142	149	155	162	169	176	182	189	196	203	236	270
70	132	139	146	153	160	167	174	181	188	195	202	207	243	278
71	136	143	150	157	165	172	179	186	193	200	208	215	250	286
72	140	147	154	162	169	177	184	191	199	206	213	221	258	294
73	144	151	159	166	174	182	189	197	204	212	219	227	265	302
74	148	155	163	171	179	186	194	202	210	218	225	233	272	311
75	152	160	168	176	184	192	200	208	216	224	232	240	279	319
76	156	164	172	180	189	197	205	213	221	230	238	246	287	328

A healthy BMI falls between 19 and 25. Above 25 indicates you may be overweight, and above 30 indicates you may be clinically obese.

The BMI is an indicator only. The only way to really know your ideal BMI requires consultation with a doctor. So use this BMI chart as a guide only. Don't worry about what the number is today—after all, that's what we are here to correct!

APPENDIX B

Success Graph

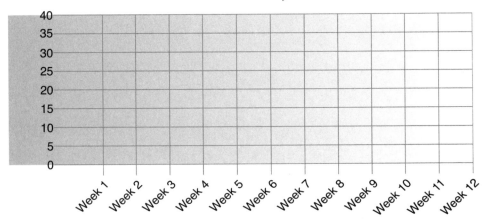

APPENDIX C

GLYCEMIC LOAD VALUES OF COMMON FOODS

The values on the following pages have been compiled from the GI listings in the July 2002 issue of the *American Journal of Clinical Nutrition* and the USDA Nutrient Database:

Sorted by Increasing GL in Food Groups	GI	Carb g	Fat g	GL Index
Beans				
Beans, soy, boiled, 1/2 cup, 90 g	18	10	7	2
Beans, lentils, green and brown, boiled, 95 g	30	16	0	5
Beans, kidney, boiled, 1/2 cup, 90 g	27	18	0	5
Beans, lentils, (average), 100 g	28	19	0	5
Beans, lima, baby, frozen, 1/2 cup, 95 g	32	17	0	5
Beans, black, soup, 220 ml	64	9	2	6
Beans, pinto, canned, 1/2 cup, 95 g	45	13	0	6
Beans, kidney, canned and drained, 1/2 cup, 95 g	52	13	0	7
Beans, broad, frozen, boiled, 1/2 cup, 120 g	79	9	1	7
Beans, black-eyed, soaked, boiled, 1/2 cup, 120 g	42	24	1	10
Bread				
Bread, sourdough, rye, 1 slice, 30 g	48	12	1	6
Bread, stone-ground whole-meal, 1 slice, 30 g	53	11	1	6
Bread, wonder, enriched white (USA), 1 slice 38 g	73	10	2	7
Bread, sourdough, wheat, 1 slice, 30 g	54	14	1	8
Bread, Home-Pride, butter top (USA), 1 slice, 38 g	38	38	38	38
Bread, pumpernickel, 1 slice, 60 g	41	21	1	9
Bread, whole-meal (wheat flour), 1 slice, 30 g	69	14	1	10
Bread, Healthy Choice, hearty 7-grain, 1 slice, 38 g	56	18	1	10
Bread, white (wheat flour), 1 slice, 30 g	70	19	1	13
Bread, Healthy Choice, 100% whole grain (USA), 1 slice 38g	62	18	1	11
Bread, Melba toast, 4 squares, 30 g	70	19	1	13
Bread, hamburger bun, 1 prepacked bun, 50 g	61	24	3	15
Bread, rye, 1 slice, 50 g	65	23	1	15
Bread, light rye, 1 slice, 50 g	68	23	1	16
Bread, croissant, 1, 50 g	67	27	14	18
Bread, pita, 1 piece, 65 g	57	38	1	22
Bread, bagel, 1, 70 g	72	35	1	25
Breakfast Cereal				
Breakfast Cereal, All-Bran 1/2 cup, 40 g	42	22	1	9
Breakfast Cereal, Special K (Aus), 1 cup, 30 g	54	21	0	11
Breakfast Cereal, shredded wheat, 1/3 cup, 25 g	67	18	0	12
Breakfast Cereal, All-Bran, Fruit 'n Oats, 1/2 cup, 45 g	39	33	2	13
Breakfast Cereal, Cheerios, 30 g	74	20	2	15
Breakfast Cereal, Honey Smacks, 3/4 cup, 30 g	56	27	1	19
Breakfast Cereal, Total, 30 g	76	22	0	17

Sorted by Increasing GL in Food Groups	GI	Carb g	Fat g	GL Index
Breakfast Cereal, Froot Loops, 1 cup, 30 g	69	27	1	19
Breakfast Cereal, Cocoa Pops, 3/4 cup, 30 g	77	26	0	20
Breakfast Cereal, Corn Chex, 30 g	83	25	0	21
Breakfast Cereal, Corn Flakes, 1 cup, 30 g	84	26	0	22
Breakfast Cereal, Rice Krispies, 1 cup, 30 g	82	27	0	22
Breakfast Cereal, Rice Chex, 1 cup, 30 g	89	25	0	22
Breakfast Cereal, Grape Nuts, 1/2 cup, 58 g	71	47	1	33
Cake				
Cake, angel food, 1 slice, 30 g	67	17	0	11
Cake, sponge, 1 slice, 60 g	46	32	4	15
Cake, Cupcake, with icing and cream filling, 1 cake, 38 g	73	26	3	19
Cake, chocolate fudge, mix, (Betty Crocker), 73 g + 33 g frosting	38	54	17	21
Cake, banana, 1 slice, 80 g	47	46	7	22
Cake, pound, 1 slice, 80 g	54	42	15	23
Crackers				
Crackers, Premium soda, 3, 25 g	74	17	4	13
Crackers, water, 5, 25 g	78	18	2	14
Crackers, rice cake, 2, 25 g	82	21	1	17
Drink				
Drink, milk, full fat, 1 cup, 250 ml	27	12	10	3
Drink, soy, So Good, 1cup, 250 ml	31	12	9	4
Drink, milk, skim, 1 cup, 250 ml	32	13	0	4
Drink, Quik, strawberry, in low-fat milk, 12 g in 250 ml milk	35	13	0	5
Drink, Nesquik, strawberry powder, 3 tsp in 250 ml milk	50	14	0	7
Drink, grapefruit juice, unsweetened, 1 cup, 250 ml	65	23	1	15
Drink, Nesquik, chocolate powder, 3 tsp in 250 ml milk	55	14	0	8
Drink, orange juice, 1 cup, 250 ml	78	15	0	12
Drink, sports drink, Gatorade, 1 cup, 250 ml	78	15	0	12
Drink, pineapple juice, unsweetened, canned 250 ml	46	27	0	12
Drink, apple juice, unsweetened, 1 cup, 250 ml	40	33	0	13
Drink, cordial, orange, diluted, 1 cup, 250 ml	66	20	0	13
Drink, cranberry juice cocktail (Ocean Spray USA) 240 ml	68	34	0	23
Drink, soft, Coca Cola, 375 ml	63	40	0	25
Drink, soft, Fanta, 375 ml	68	51	0	35
Drink, milk, sweetened condensed, 1/2 cup, 160 g	61	90	15	55
Fruit				
Fruit, grapefruit, raw, 1/2 medium, 100 g	25	5	0	1

Sorted by Increasing GL in Food Groups	GI	Carb g	Fat g	GL Index
Fruit, cherries, 20, 80 g	22	10	0	2
Fruit, plums, 3–4 small, 100 g	39	7	0	3
Fruit, peach, fresh, 1 large, 110 g	42	7	0	3
Fruit, pear, canned, SPC Lite, 3 halves	25	15	0	4
Fruit, apricots, fresh, 3 medium, 100 g	57	7	0	4
Fruit, apricots, dried, 5–6 pieces, 30 g	31	13	0	4
Fruit, kiwi fruit, 1 raw, peeled, 80 g	52	8	0	4
Fruit, orange, 1 medium, 130 g	52	8	0	4
Fruit, peach, canned in natural juice, 1/2 cup, 125 g	38	12	0	5
Fruit, pear, canned in pear juice, 1/2 cup, 150 g	43	13	0	6
Fruit, watermelon, 1 cup, 150 g	72	8	0	6
Fruit, pineapple, fresh, 2 slices, 125 g	66	10	0	7
Fruit, apple, 1 medium, 150 g	38	18	0	7
Fruit, grapes, green, 1 cup, 100 g	46	15	0	7
Fruit, prunes, pitted, 6, 40 g	29	25	0	7
Fruit, fruit cocktail, canned in natural juice, 1/2 cup, 125 g	55	15	0	8
Fruit, apricots, canned in light syrup, 1/2 cup, 125 g	64	13	0	8
Fruit, peach, canned in light syrup, 1/2 cup, 125 g	52	18	0	9
Fruit, mango, 1 small, 150 g	55	19	0	10
Fruit, figs, dried, tenderised (water added), 50 g	61	22	1	13
Fruit, banana, raw, 1 medium, 150 g	55	32	0	18
Fruit, raisins, 1/4 cup, 40 g	64	28	0	18
Fruit, dates, dried, 5, 40 g	103	27	0	28
Grains				
Grains, rice bran, extruded, 1 tablespoon, 10 g	19	3	2	1
Grains, barley, pearled, boiled, 1/2 cup, 80 g	25	17	1	4
Grains, bulgur, cooked, 2/3 cup, 120 g	48	22	1	11
Grains, couscous, cooked, 2/3 cup, 120 g	65	28	0	18
Grains, buckwheat, cooked, 1/2 cup, 80 g	54	57	3	31
Grains, rice, instant, cooked, 1 cup, 180 g	87	38	0	33
Grains, rice, glutinous, white, steamed, 1 cup, 174 g	98	37	0	36
Grains, tapioca (boiled with milk), 1 cup, 265 g	81	51	11	41
Ice Cream				
Ice cream, full-fat, 2 scoops, 50 g	61	10	6	6
Ice cream, low-fat, 2 scoops, 50 g	50	13	2	7
Muffins				
Muffins, banana, oat and honey, from mix, 50 g	65	28	4	18

Sorted by Increasing GL in Food Groups	GI	Carb g	Fat g	GL Index
Muffins, apple, 1 muffin, 80 g	44	44	10	19
Muffins, bran, 1 muffin, 80 g	60	34	8	20
Muffins, blueberry, 1 muffin, 80 g	59	41	8	24
Pasta				
Pasta, tortellini, cheese, cooked, 180 grams	50	21	8	11
Pasta, Ravioli, meat filled, cooked, 1 cup, 180 g	39	30	11	12
Pasta, vermicelli, cooked, 1 cup, 180 g	35	45	0	16
Pasta, spaghetti, gluten-free in tomato sauce, 1 small tin, 220 g	68	27	1	18
Pasta, macaroni and cheese, packaged, cooked, 220 g	64	30	24	19
Pasta, spaghetti, white, cooked, 1 cup, 180 g	41	56	1	23
Pasta, macaroni, cooked, 1 cup, 180 g	45	56	1	25
Pasta, noodles, 2-minute, cooked, dry, 85 g	46	55	16	25
Pasta, linguine, thick, cooked, 1 cup, 180 g	46	56	1	26
Peas				
Peas, dried, boiled, 1/2 cup, 70 g	22	4	0	1
Peas, green, fresh, frozen, boiled, 1/2 cup, 80 g	48	5	0	2
Peas, chick, canned, drained, 1/2 cup, 95 g	42	15	2	6
Peas, chick, boiled, 120 g	33	22	3	7
Sugar				
Sugar, fructose, 10 g	23	10	0	2
Sugar, lactose, 10 g	46	10	0	5
Sugar, sucrose, 10 g	65	10	0	7
Sugar, glucose, 10 g	102	10	0	10
Sugar, maltose, 10 g	105	10	0	11
Pudding				
Pudding, instant, vanilla, mix, full cream, 100 g	41	16	4	7
Pudding, instant, chocolate, mix, full cream, 100 g	49	16	4	8
Snack				
Snack, peanuts, roasted, salted, 1/2 cup, 75 g	14	11	40	2
Snack, popcorn, low-fat, 2 cups (popped), 20 g	55	10	2	6
Snack, Life Savers, 5, peppermint, 10 g	70	10	0	7
Snack, jelly beans, 5, 10 g	80	9	0	7
Snack, chicken nuggets, 100 g	46	17	16	8
Snack, M&M's, (peanut), 50 g	33	30	13	10
Snack, Kudos, (whole grain bars, choc chip), 30 g	62	19	5	12
Snack, donut with cinnamon and sugar, 40 g	76	16	8	12
Snack, English muffin, bread, 1 slice, 34 g	77	16	1	12

Sorted by Increasing GL in Food Groups	GI	Carb g	Fat g	GL Index
Snack, Roll-Ups, 1	99	13	1	13
Snack, potato chips, plain, 50 g	54	24	16	13
Snack, corn chips, Doritos original, 50 g	42	33	11	14
Snack, Snickers, 59 g	41	35	14	14
Snack, pizza, Super Supreme (Pizza Hut), thin & crispy, 2 slices, 204 g	30	50	27	15
Snack, Twix, cookie bar (caramel), 59 g	44	34	14	16
Snack, pretzels, 50 g	83	22	1	18
Snack, cheese twists, 50 g	74	29	15	21
Snack, Pop-Tarts, double choc, 50 g	70	36	5	25
Snack, pizza, Super Supreme, pan, 2 slices, 268 g	36	72	31	26
Snack, Mars Bar, 60 g	65	41	11	27
Snack, Skittles, 62 g	70	55	3	39
Soups				
Soups, tomato, canned, 220 ml	38	15	1	6
Soups, black bean, 220 ml	64	9	2	6
Soups, lentil, canned, 220 ml	44	14	0	6
Soups, split pea, canned, ready to serve, 220 ml	60	13	2	8
Soups, green pea, canned, ready to serve, 220 ml	66	22	1	15
Vegetable				
Vegetable, carrots, peeled, boiled, 1/2 cup, 85 g	49	3	0	1
Vegetable, pumpkin, peeled, boiled, 1/2 cup, 85 g	75	6	0	5
Vegetable, parsnips, boiled, 1/2 cup, 75 g	97	8	0	8
Vegetable, sweet potato, peeled, boiled, 80 g	54	16	0	9
Vegetable, sweet corn, 1/2 cup, 80 g	55	18	1	10
Vegetable, potatoes, new, canned, drained, 5 small, 175 g	65	21	0	14
Vegetable, potatoes, baked in oven (no fat), 1 medium, 120 g	93	15	0	14
Vegetable, potatoes, mashed, 1/2 cup, 120 g	91	16	0	15
Vegetable, potatoes, instant, prepared, 1/2 cup	83	18	1	15
Vegetable, potatoes, French fries, fine cut, small serving, 120 g	75	49	26	37
Yogurt				
Yogurt, low-fat, artificial sweetener, 200 g	14	12	0	2
Yogurt, low-fat, fruit, 200 g	33	26	0	9

APPENDIX D

Hit the Bull's-Eye!

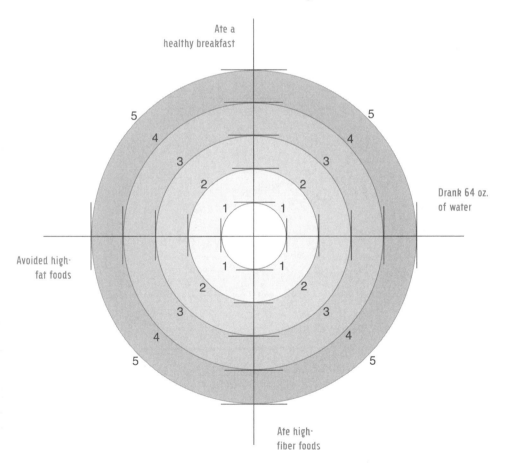

APPENDIX E

Action Sheet		
Activities that replace or postpone eating	Desired food	Outcome and assessment
	date_____	
	date_____	
	date_____	
	date_____	
	date_____	

APPENDIX F

My Food Revision Chart	
Original Ingredients	Fit and Faithful Ingredients

APPENDIX G

Make a copy of the chart on the following page, and use it to plan your meals each week. Search for recipes with a low Glycemic Index (try your local library or the Internet), and find dishes for each meal on the chart.

Weekly Meal Planner

		Sunday	Monday	Tuesday	Wednesday	Thursday	Friday	Saturday
Breakfast	Grain Cereal							
	Liquid							
	Other							
Lunch	Main Dish							
	Side Dish(es)							
	Beverage/Other							
Dinner	Main Dish							
	Side Dish(es)							
	Beverage/Other							
Snack	Midmorning Snack							
	Evening Snack							

APPENDIX H

Daily Meal Planner	
Breakfast	
Midmorning Snack	
Lunch	
Afternoon Snack	
Dinner	
End of the Day Treat	

APPENDIX I

THE NEW FOOD PYRAMID

Red meat and butter
IN LIMITED QUANTITIES

White rice, white bread, potatoes, pasta, and sweets
IN LIMITED QUANTITIES

Dairy products and calcium supplements
1–2 PORTIONS A DAY

Vitamin supplements
FOR ALMOST EVERYBODY

Fish, poultry, and eggs
0–2 PORTIONS A DAY

Alcoholic drinks
MODERATE COMSUMPTION

Nuts and pulses
1–3 PORTIONS A DAY

Vegetables
IN ABUNDANCE

Fruit
2–3 PORTIONS A DAY

Whole-meal foods
ALWAYS

Vegetable oils
AT ALMOST EVERY MEAL
(soys, corn, sunflower, olive, peanut, etc.)

DAILY PHYSICAL EXERCISE AND WEIGHT CONTROL

APPENDIX J

The Summarized AWE Chart

avoid	watch	eat
Snacks		
High-sugar soft drinks	Sherbets	Frozen grapes and berries
Packaged sweets	Low-fat ice creams	Lite yogurts
Fried chips, etc.	"Energy" bars	Sugar-free pudding (Pudding Pops)
Chocolate and candy bars	Fruit juices (frozen fruit-juice pops)	A bowl of high-grain cereal
Cookies	Baked chips	
Diet sodas		
Cakes and pastries		

avoid	watch	eat
Beverages		
High-sugar soft drinks	Coffee	Pure water
Alcohol	Black tea	Green teas
Diet sodas	Wine	
	Flavored water	
	Fruit juices	
Fats and Oils		
Coconut oil	Corn oil	Olive oil
Palm kernel	Peanut oil	Canola oil
Hydrogenated oils	Safflower oil	Fish oil
Partially hydrogenated oils	Sesame oil	Soybean oil
	Sunflower oil	
Margarine		
Butter		
Dairy Products		
Whole milk	Low-fat milk	Plain yogurt
Soft cheese	Hard cheeses	Skim (nonfat) milk
Processed cheese foods	Ice milk (nonfat)	
Ice Cream		

avoid	watch	eat

Meats and Proteins

Fatty red meat and pork	Lean red meat	Fish (especially those high in Omega-3 fats)
Processed meats, like bacon and sausage	Nuts	Dried beans
	Black-eyed peas	
Meats cooked with the skin	Lima beans	Soy protein
		Lentils
	Eggs	
		Free-range poultry

Vegetables

Starchy vegetables (Potatoes)	Sweet potatoes	Green vegetables
		Carrots
Deep-fried vegetables		
		Most nonstarchy vegetables

Fruits

Dates, figs, raisins (high GL value)	Bananas	Melons
Avocados	Orange juice	Apples
	Any juices with sweeteners added and/or pulp removed	Most other fruits have a good GL rating (check the chart in appendix C to be sure)

avoid	watch	eat
Grains, Breads, and Related Foods		
Breads made with high amounts of fat, oils, butter, etc. (e.g., fast food or canned biscuits)	White rice	Whole grains
	Bagels	Whole-grain brown rice
Nonenriched white flour	English muffins	Bran crackers
Sugary breakfast cereals	Muffins	Whole-grain breads
White rice		Whole-grain breakfast cereals
Sweet breads		Pitas, tortillas, and other flat breads (especially whole grain)

NOTES

Week 1: Transformation

1. From http://www.pueblo.gsa.gov/cic_text/food/food-pyramid /main.htm. For more information, contact USDA's Center for Nutrition Policy and Promotion: U.S. Department of Agriculture Center for Nutrition Policy and Promotion, 1120 20th St., NW, Suite 200, North Lobby, Washington, DC 20036-3475.

Week 2: Charting the Path

1. From http://www.eatrightpa.org (Pennsylvania Dietetic Association).

Week 3: Your New Body

1. From http://www. auschwitz.dk/kolbe.htm.
2. From *International Journal of Obesity & Related Metabolic Disorders,* 23(11):1151–59, 1999.
3. See "Know your Fats" at http://www.americanheart.org, the American Heart Association Web site.

Week 5: Your New Spirit

1. Based on data from *International Table of Glycemic Index and Glycemic Load Values: 2002,* Kaye Foster-Powell, Susanna

HA Holt, and Janette C Brand-Miller, AJCN, Vol.76, No.1, 5–56, July 2002.

Week 7: Food, Fitness, and the Father

1. Ellen W. Cutler, *The Food Allergy Cure: A New Solution to Food Cravings, Obesity, Depression, Headaches, Arthritis, and Fatigue* (New York: Three Rivers Press, April 2003).

Week 9: Living with Others

1. Graham Kerr, *Graham Kerr's Best: A Low-Fat, Heart Healthy Cookbook* (Itasca, Ill.: Putnam Publishing Group, November 2000).
2. Greg Jantz, *Too Close to the Flame* (West Monroe, La.: Howard Publishing, 1999).
3. Jeff Prugh, *Herschel Walker* (Greenwich, Conn.: Fawcett, 1983).

Week 10: Living with God, Living with Hope!

1. For an excellent book on the subject of spiritual growth, see *How People Grow*, by Dr. Henry Cloud and Dr. John Townsend.

Week 11: Reaping the Harvest

1. See *The Legend of the Starfish*, http://216.71.2.132/texts /topics/makeadifference/legendofstarfish.shtml.
2. "Sugar on the Brain," from http://www.princeton .edu/pr/news/02/q2/0620-hoebel.com.
3. Recipes for Spicy Pita Chips and Shirred Egg Supreme are taken from the Web site http://www.naturalhealthdoc.net. Used by permission.

Week 12: Transformation—Reborn

1. Walter C. Willett and Meir J. Stampfer, "Rebuilding the Food Pyramid," *Scientific American* (January 2003).

Appendices

    1. From the July 2002 issue of the *American Journal of Clinical Nutrition* and the USDA Nutrient Database.

    For further information on the Center for Counseling and Health Resources, go to: www.aplaceofhope.com

or

The Center, Inc.
PO Box 700
547 Dayton Street
Edmonds, WA 98020
Nationwide toll free 888-771-5166
Fax 425-670-2807